The Essential Guide to Personal Finance for Teens and College Students

Practical Hacks to Eliminate Money-Stress and Build Wealth for the Future

Joshua Rivedal

Skookum Hill Publishing and The i'Mpossible Project

PHILADELPHIA, PA

Copyright © 2023 by Joshua Rivedal

The content contained within this book may not be reproduced, duplicated, or transmitted without direct written permission from the author or the publisher.

Under no circumstances will any blame or legal responsibility be held against the publisher, or author, for any damages, reparation, or monetary loss due to the information contained within this book, either directly or indirectly.

Legal Notice:
This book is copyright protected. It is only for personal use. You cannot amend, distribute, sell, use, quote or paraphrase any part, or the content within this book, without the consent of the author or publisher.

Disclaimer Notice:
Please note the information contained within this document is for educational and entertainment purposes only. All effort has been executed to present accurate, up to date, reliable, complete information. No warranties of any kind are declared or implied. Readers acknowledge that the author is not engaged in the rendering of legal, financial, medical, or professional advice. The content within this book has been derived from various sources. Please consult a licensed professional before attempting any techniques outlined in this book.

By reading this document, the reader agrees that under no circumstances is the author responsible for any losses, direct or indirect, that are incurred as a result of the use of the information contained within this document, including, but not limited to, errors, omissions, or inaccuracies.

Book cover design, format, and layout – Rachel Bostwick

The Essential Guide to Personal Finance for Teens and College Students - *Practical Hacks to Eliminate Money-Stress and Build Wealth for the Future* / Joshua Rivedal. -- 1st ed.

ISBN 978-1-7356171-4-5

CONTENTS

INTRODUCTION 1
CHAPTER 1: LET'S TALK ABOUT FINANCE 5
CHAPTER 2: HOW TO THINK ABOUT MONEY 13
CHAPTER 3: MAKING MONEY 23
CHAPTER 4: WHERE TO STORE YOUR MONEY 31
CHAPTER 5: BUDGETING BASICS 47
CHAPTER 6: MANAGING CREDIT 55
CHAPTER 7: DEALING WITH DEBT 63
CHAPTER 8: SAVING THE RIGHT WAY 69
CHAPTER 9: THE POWER OF INVESTING 79
CHAPTER 10: WHAT ABOUT TAXES? 87
CHAPTER 11: PLANNING FOR RAINY DAYS 95
CHAPTER 12: BUILDING A FUTURE OF WEALTH 99
REFERENCES 103
ABOUT THE AUTHOR 115

INTRODUCTION

"It is health that is real wealth. And not pieces of gold and silver."
– Mahatma Gandhi

Are you tired of feeling like you're still being treated like a little kid, even though you feel ready to take on the world? I get it. It's frustrating to be seen as someone who doesn't have a grip on their own life, even though you know you're capable of so much more! I'll let you in on a little secret: gaining your independence and living your best life lies in becoming financially self-reliant *and* being proactive about your mental well-being. The two actually go hand-in-hand. Let's talk about the financial part.

Unfortunately, not many young adults know where to start when it comes to establishing their financial independence. Not to call anyone out, but research found that most teenagers (74%) don't feel confident about personal finance.[1] A scary statistic, for sure, but that's where this book comes in. It's a practical and helpful resource written for someone (like you) who wants to plan for their future. You're not alone in your search for reliable information and guidance on personal finance. So many resources out there are way too complicated or not tailored to your needs. In this book, I'll share the secrets to making money and building long-term wealth. You'll gain the confidence and knowledge to handle your finances like a pro, putting you on the path to financial independence. I'll also talk a wee bit about mental well-being and how it's tied to financial wellness and a healthier future.

WHO AM I, AND WHY AM I THE GUY TO WRITE THIS BOOK?

I'm Joshua Rivedal, and I've got a good reason for wanting to help you master your finances. This quick story starts when I was a freshman in high school—the first time I can remember anything involving money or finance being important. I was experiencing some major trauma at home at the hands of my father; my mental health was suffering tremendously and had been deteriorating for some time. I knew I couldn't live like this any longer. But where would I go, and what would I do? I was too young to drive a car, but I was keenly aware that a vehicle would be my eventual ticket to freedom. My family wasn't financially well-off, so I'd need a job to purchase a car and pay all the expenses that went along with it.

Fortunately, I was old enough to get a job. And that summer, I started work at Six Flags in New Jersey (which was amazing, by the way!). I rarely spent the money I earned; I learned early on that spending on clothes, food, and candy I didn't need wasn't going to win me my freedom. I worked hard every summer in high school, and by my junior year, I had enough money to buy a used car from my friend's father. I also had to have enough money for gas and insurance, so I made a little list (what I later learned was a "budget") to make sure I was *earning enough and saving enough to meet my goals*.

Fast forward a little, and by age nineteen, I saved enough to meet my ultimate objective; to move out of my father's house and in with a friend. It was then that I could pursue my dreams—I wanted to sing in old-timey musicals on Broadway—and work toward living my best life. And much of my early success can be attributed to paying attention to personal finance.

That was more than twenty years ago, and these days I'm an international public speaker, educator, comic, and author… and working hard to live mentally well…and I am! I have a background in business (with a strong focus in finance and economics) and in speaking at a lot of colleges, high schools, and workplaces about suicide prevention and mental health. In my life and my work, I've come to realize that financial well-being is closely linked to mental wellness. Chronic stress can cloud our judgment and have damaging consequences for our financial affairs.[2] That's because making healthy financial decisions, or any decisions for that matter, becomes extra hard when we feel overly stressed. Unchecked stress breeds more stress, and it turns into a vicious cycle that can spiral out of control. The key to avoiding stressful financial situations is to develop strong personal finance habits. If budgeting becomes second nature, debt will no longer be a burden. Saving money and investing will feel as natural as breathing.

This Book Is For You (Yes, You!)

Money matters, and it can have a profound impact on our daily lives and relationships. Financial stress often goes hand in hand with mental health challenges, which is why it is essential to take control of your financial future. Just look at the current state of the world! Financial hardship has become more prevalent, leaving some people unable to access health care.[3] But don't lose hope; it's never too late to start taking care of your finances. It's a good idea to start early, as you'll be better off in the future.

By the end of this journey, you'll have a solid foundation of financial knowledge that will serve you well. That's because you'll be equipped to avoid the common pitfalls and mistakes that so many young people make. I've been there. I've made financial mistakes, too (sigh). I've seen firsthand how financial struggles can eat away at mental health. That's why I'm committed to helping people like you. So, if you are ready to transform your life, come with me on a journey that will break the shackles of financial stress. Get ready for a solid financial education that can also serve as *a* tool to enhance your overall well-being. Are you excited? I sure am!

CHAPTER 1

LET'S TALK ABOUT FINANCE

Personal finance, or the process of planning and managing financial activities like spending, saving, investing, and income generation, can be difficult to navigate.[4] Where do you even begin? Here's a little tip: The most important thing to remember when learning about personal finance is simply to make time for it. Take advantage of any resources you may have, especially books, which are excellent starting points. Keep in mind that without personal finance knowledge, we would be working all our lives and never getting ahead.

What, then, is personal finance? To put it simply, it is how we handle our finances.[5] But that's not really a complete definition. There are several aspects of personal finance that must be managed, including...

- **Income:** Whether you earn a few dollars from a side job or have multiple income streams pouring liquid gold into your pockets (I wish that were a thing!), you must manage your income sources carefully. That's because there are taxes to pay, retirement contributions (you're never too young to think about that), and health insurance deductions that need to be considered. Gross pay does not equal what you actually get to take home. There are always taxes to pay and insurance to cover, so your after-tax pay is always lower than your pre-tax pay.
- **Spending:** If you can't resist the urge to splurge, then money management skills are essential. Taking the time to teach yourself these skills will help you understand your monthly expenses much better and can help you stick to a budget (more on budgeting in Chapter 5).
- **Saving:** Putting a few dollars away for a rainy day can be a lifesaver in times of emergency and can prevent many people from going into debt in the first place. Contrary to popular belief, you don't need to earn huge stacks of cash to be able to save! By sharpening your personal finance skills, you'll be able to find creative ways to save, even when you're not making a lot of money. So, teaching yourself the art of saving is incredibly useful.
- **Investing:** When you want to grow your money for the future or reach a financial goal quicker, investing can be a good option. There are many ways to invest, but you'll need to educate yourself and receive sound financial advice to help you select the right type of investments for your needs and goals.
- **Debt:** When you are ready to buy cars, houses, or a business, debt becomes an inevitable reality. Keep in mind that when you

take on debt, it is vital to understand how it will affect your spending. Debt has to be managed wisely, otherwise, it can trap us in an endless cycle of one financial crisis after another. It is best to put money aside for major purchases if you can.
- **Insurance:** Policies and insurance coverage are a key part of a good personal finance plan and can provide peace of mind in many situations.

As you can see, "personal finance" has a pretty broad scope and impacts every part of our lives. I'm pretty certain nobody wants to go through life with permanent money worries, so it's a little troubling that most adults (64%) admit that money is a major source of stress for them.[6] It's never too late to take charge of your financial future, but young adults can learn valuable personal finance lessons in a safe space, helping them tackle money matters with confidence later in life.

At home, teens can make their own money decisions, just like my friend's daughter, LaKeisha, who had her heart set on buying her first car. She found a summer job and discovered that she'd save $7 a day if she packed a lunch. Of course, $7 a day did not seem like much at first, but LaKeisha's savings grew over time. LaKeisha's parents noticed how she started with her savings plan and encouraged her to stick to it so she could see how the savings added up in real time.

LaKeisha got her car because she took the time to gain hands-on experience managing her money. Gaining that experience was a great confidence booster and helped her succeed. But there's another reason why gaining hands-on experience early on is so important; it is one of the key drivers for financial well-being in adulthood![7]

WHY PERSONAL FINANCE MATTERS

When it comes to your finances, remember this: You are in control. And you're already on the right track by wanting to learn more. Personal finance matters because having money management skills is important for a healthy, secure, and happy life.[8]

Here's something interesting: The relationship we have with money can be healthy or unhealthy. Some people may see money in a negative light, especially if they haven't had the greatest money role models. The nice thing is that this relationship can change when we have a better understanding of financial principles. This empowers us to create a better financial path for ourselves and to have a positive perception of money.

When we understand money management, we give ourselves the power of choice. Think about it for a second. If we know how credit scores work (more on this in Chapter 6) and do our bit to maintain a good score, we'll have a much easier time getting loans and leases when we truly need them. Financial stability is a major reason why everyone should take personal finance seriously.

Now, let's talk about what happens when we don't understand how our finances work. Spoiler alert: It's going to be a bumpy ride.

- **Feeling stressed out:** A lack of financial knowledge can have a major impact on your life. Adults find that finances are often a major cause of stress, which can have a negative impact on their overall psychological health.[9] This, in turn, reduces the quality of our lives. Without basic personal finance knowledge, you can easily get yourself into a sticky, stressful money mess.
- **Living with maxed-out credit cards:** Unmanageable debt is a common problem. It can happen when you max out credit cards, miss loan payments, or struggle to keep up with bills. It's not a fun place to be and can impact your future and mental health in the long run.
- **Saving becomes incredibly hard:** Imagine not having enough money to cover a $400 emergency. That's a reality that 37% of Americans face.[10] Not having any savings often leads people to take on more debt to deal with unexpected expenses.
- **Financial stress can even affect your health:** People who constantly worry about money are more likely to have poor health and even experience depression.[11] It's especially tough for

communities that face financial insecurity. Financial stress can even increase the risk of heart disease.[12]

- **Bankruptcy can become a reality:** Bankruptcy is no joke. It's a tough situation that can have lasting consequences for your financial profile. It can take years to rebuild credit after bankruptcy. It is a real struggle, whether due to a lack of financial knowledge, poor decisions, or unexpected emergencies like hospital bills.

But here's the thing: By wanting to learn about personal finance, you are already taking the right steps. It is possible to avoid these issues and build a better financial future with the right knowledge and skills. So, continue to learn, and do not be afraid to take charge of your financial future. You can do it.

Personal Finance 101:
Teaching Yourself About Money

Want to dive into the world of finance, but are not sure where to start? Don't worry! The good news is that there's a ton of information out there, so getting started couldn't be easier. Whether you are a teenager, preparing for college, a full-time student, or taking a gap year, learning about personal finance is within your reach. You can start your online search on platforms like YouTube and podcasts that cover financial topics.[13] You can also check out numerous free podcasts that cover financial topics. They are easy to download and often help simplify complex financial concepts. Try watching interviews with well-known financial and money experts and reading personal finance blogs and books based on your goals. Just know that the advice you find may not be tailored to your specific goals, and the person giving it might not be a licensed financial professional.

Apart from online resources, you shouldn't overlook traditional ways of building your financial knowledge. Your local library, bookstore, or online retailer offers an extensive selection of books on every imaginable financial topic.

Take a Finance Course

To deepen your understanding of finance, consider enrolling in in-person or online courses. Many universities offer free or paid online courses you can take at your convenience. If you've made it this far, you're clearly serious about your financial journey. Now, it's time to make learning a daily habit. Subscribing to publications like *The Wall Street Journal* will give you a daily overview of global business operations, including a fantastic Personal Finance section. *Barron's* is another respected publication in the financial services industry. Find a publication that matches your interests and dive into it regularly.

Talk to Experts and Professionals

Once you have a solid understanding of various financial aspects, it's time to seek advice from experts. Financial services professionals, such as financial advisors, bankers, accountants, and attorneys, make a living out of their expertise and can guide you in managing student debt, finding suitable mortgages, and more. You can attend seminars, have one-on-one consultations, or simply engage in informal conversations. Many professionals are happy to share their knowledge with those who show a keen interest in learning.

Money Tools Make Things Easier

The right tools can help make your personal finance journey easier and more successful. Here are some money tools that can help:

- **Budgeting apps:** Budgeting is a crucial skill that everyone should learn early on. Budgeting apps can make it easy to track your income and offer personalized suggestions to help you stay on track and make smarter spending choices.
- **Saving and investing apps:** As a young adult, you may want to start saving and investing for the future. Apps like Acorns or Stash can be great companions on this journey. They offer easy ways to set aside small amounts of money and invest them in

diversified portfolios. These apps often round up your purchases to the nearest dollar and invest the spare change automatically, helping your savings grow over time (they do take a small piece, so make sure you read the fine print).

- **Expense-tracking apps:** Keeping tabs on your spending is crucial to understanding where your money is going and making necessary adjustments. Expense-tracking apps allow you to categorize your expenses, track your spending patterns, and even split bills and expenses with friends or roommates. By having a clear picture of your spending habits, you can identify areas where you can cut back and save more.

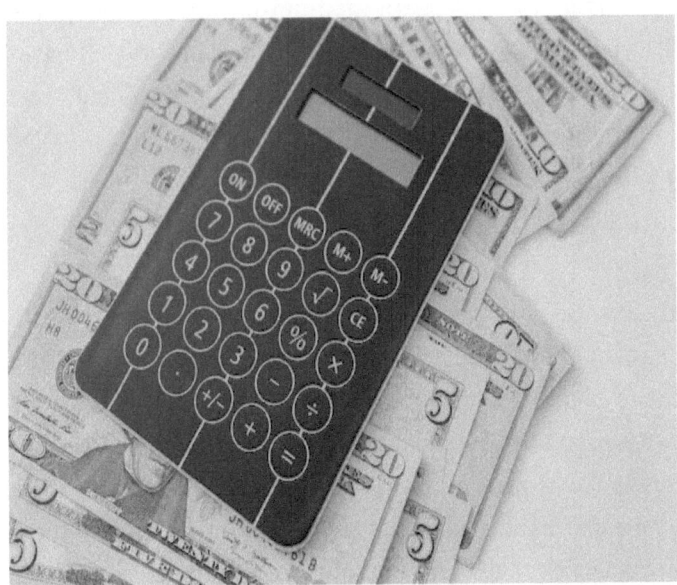

Reflection Questions

- What are the basics of personal finance?
- Why is it important to understand how to manage your money?

Exercise – Daydreaming About Money (Kinda)

Sure, a goal without a plan is just a wish, but in this exercise, all you have to do is dream big. We're not setting goals because we haven't yet gotten to all the necessary financial concepts to set you up for success (more on that in later chapters). But by allowing yourself to dream a bit, you're giving yourself permission to think big and envision what's possible.

Reflect on Financial Dreams. Take a few minutes (or as long as you want) to think about your financial dreams—in the short-term (a few months up to 1-2 years), medium-term (3-5 years), and long-term (10+ years). Write down at least one dream for each time frame. These can include saving for education, buying a car, owning a home, or retirement planning.

That's it!

Putting It All Together

Personal finance involves income management, spending, saving, investing, debt management, and insurance. This makes it all the more important to change the way we think about money. With a growth mindset, learning about personal finance becomes much easier. Try to seek knowledge from different sources and spend time developing healthy financial habits (such as saving and budgeting). Money tools such as budgeting apps, saving and investing apps, and expense-tracking apps can be very helpful. Don't hesitate to use them. It's all part of changing the way we think about money and adopting a healthy money mindset, but we'll talk more about that in the next chapter.

CHAPTER 2

HOW TO THINK ABOUT MONEY

Changing your money mindset can provide a greater sense of freedom, security, and peace of mind. This can involve anything from reframing your thoughts about money to taking practical steps toward financial management and planning.

Questioning Spending Habits: A Note From My Friend, Jen

Up until a few years ago, my friend Jen always had money problems. That's when she started to question what she was spending her money on. Did she really need four pairs of sunglasses, a laptop, a tablet, and a closet bursting with clothes she hardly wore? Did she truly need to get a new phone every year or splurge on the latest gaming gadget? Jen was living her best life (kinda), but something felt off. No matter how hard she worked and how much money Jen earned, those greenbacks evaporated just as quickly. Then it dawned on her: Her relationship with money was holding her back. Jen was so focused on making money that she mindlessly blew it on stuff that didn't matter to her. She tried so many times to change her spending habits, but Jen only succeeded when she changed her money mindset.

The money mindset is all about being aware of your finances and spending habits. Paying attention to how you feel, think, and react to everything around you, including your spending habits and money, is a good thing. When we're drowning in debt or struggling to make a tight budget work, we tend to make decisions that make things worse.[14] Unfortunately, people often allow their emotions and impulses to drive their spending habits without even realizing it.[15]

After digging deep with Jen about her money issues, it hit me that many of us are not living our best lives because we're spending our money on things that don't matter.

Think about it. How many times have you bought something that you absolutely adore? Or do you find yourself buying things you only *kind of* like because you crave instant gratification? For me, it was an eye-opener. I used to believe that traveling was way too expensive, so I never made any plans to go abroad. But one day, I added up how much I spent on eating out over a few months. It totaled enough to take a cool road trip and then some! Talk about a wake-up call.

Spend On Loves, Not Likes

Over the past few years, as I've changed my own money mindset, I've come up with a spending process based on loving, needing, wanting, and liking. It's really simple and a game-changer. If I don't absolutely love something, I ask myself if it is something I need, want, or just kind of like. By taking a few moments to figure out how I'm feeling about my purchase, I can prioritize how I spend that hard-earned cash. The most important thing is this: Spend the most money on what you truly need and love and cut back on the things you merely want.[16]

Love always comes first. There are tons of things I like, but I only truly want a few of them. And there are things I need that I have to prioritize over my likes. But above all else, I make sure to spend on what I genuinely love.

Basically, you need to align your spending with what genuinely matters to you. Being money-mindful means knowing what you love and being aware of your vision for life while understanding your financial situation. It's as simple as this: You work to earn money, so make sure you're spending it on things you genuinely love. So, ask yourself: Are you spending to create a life you love or just settling for a life you sort of like?

Determining Needs

So, now that you understand why changing your money mindset matters, it's time to figure out how to separate your wants from your needs. It can get a bit tricky because everyone's needs and wants can be different. Sometimes, we get so used to something that we think they're needs when they're actually wants. But don't worry, separating your expenses into wants and needs is not complicated and can help you master your finances like a boss. Here's what you need to know:
- Needs are the things you can't live without, like having a roof over your head and food in your belly.[17]

- Wants are the things that are nice to have, but you could survive without them. Think entertainment or gym memberships.

Now if you want to really rock your budget game, try the 50/30/20 budgeting method. It's really easy to do. All you need to do is to split your after-tax income like this:

- 50% goes toward your needs (think of the essentials like food, utility bills, healthcare, medication, and commuting expenses).
- 30% goes toward your wants (entertainment, dining out, travel, electronics, subscriptions, clothing, and other nonessential items fall in this category).
- 20% goes toward savings and paying off debt.

This way, you make room for both your needs and wants while also building up your savings. Sure, sometimes the line between needs and wants can get a bit blurry. It happens! Here are a few reasons why:

- **Lifestyle:** It depends on how and why you use something. For example, home internet could be a need if you work from home, but if you only use it to watch live streams or play games, it becomes more of a want.
- **Split expenses:** Some expenses have both needs and wants mixed in. Take your grocery bill, for example. Food is a need, but if you're also buying snacks and sodas, those fall into the "want" category.
- **Choices:** Sometimes, an expense is a need, but you have choices within that category. Let's say you need a phone for communication and important stuff. You can get a basic phone and fulfill that need. But if you decide to splurge on an extra-fancy smartphone just because everyone else you know has one, that extra expense becomes a "want".

Don't get me wrong—there's nothing wrong with spoiling yourself. Wants are not the enemy here. They can bring joy and help you achieve important goals like staying connected with loved ones, having fun, or taking care of your well-being. But they're not essential for survival.

ABUNDANCE VS. SCARCITY

When you hear the word "money" or "finance," what's the first thing you think about? Depending on your mindset, that answer can vary greatly. If you nurture an abundance mindset, then it's likely your attitude toward money is like having a positive outlook on life. You see opportunities and believe that you'll always have what you need. It's not just about money but also about other things like food, space, and resources. We could think of abundance as feeling satisfied with what we have and knowing there's always more when we need it.

On the other hand, if you have a scarcity mindset, things may look less rose-colored. Society frequently instills in us the belief that we never have enough and that there is not enough to go around. It can cause us to be concerned about money, hoard what we have, and be afraid of losing everything. It's a scary place to be.

But... people can change how they think and feel about something. A person's mindset is not set in stone; it exists on a spectrum and can change over time.[18]

How we think and feel about something can influence how we behave around it. The same applies to money, which is why understanding your mindset toward it is so important. By understanding how you truly think and feel about money and personal finance, you can address any limiting beliefs or negative patterns that may hold you back.

You might be wondering if you really need to change your money mindset, and the truth is, it's entirely up to you. If your current mindset works for you and aligns with your goals, that's great! But if you suspect that your mindset may be holding you back or is no longer serving you, it could be time for a change.[19]

CHANGING MONEY MINDSETS

So, how can a person change their mindset if it's not working for them? Well, the first and most important step is to pay attention to mental health. Mental health (more on that in Chapter 9) plays a huge role in how we view and use our money, so if we're not paying attention to our mental health, then our finances may suffer as a result.[20] With that being said, let's take a closer look at the things you can do to change how you think and feel about personal finance.

- **Do some detective work:** Investigate your relationship with money. Think about your beliefs, experiences, and habits around money. Consider your financial decisions, goals, and any resistance you feel. By understanding where you're coming from, you can gain clarity on your current mindset.
- **Send limiting beliefs packing:** Take a closer look at the beliefs you've uncovered about money. Are any of these ideas preventing you from achieving your goals? Which of these beliefs are helping you achieve your goals? Write them down and

think about how they've shaped the way you think about money. Now challenge those limiting beliefs and rewrite the story you tell yourself about personal finance and money. Be patient with this step—changing the way we think about something takes time, but it can be done!

- **Time is just an illusion:** An obstacle to developing a positive financial mindset is the notion that we're still young and have plenty of time to worry about finances later. This mindset can lead to procrastinating and neglecting financial education and management. But the earlier we start building healthier financial habits, the better equipped we'll be to navigate the future.
- **Remind yourself:** When learning a new habit, repetition is key. It can be useful to create affirmations or leave reminders that will reinforce your new beliefs. Say them out loud, write them down, or create visual reminders like posters or sticky notes. Remind yourself daily that you are worthy (because you are!), that there's always enough, and that you have the power to create the life you want.
- **Find new perspectives:** Knowledge can give us the power to change the way we think about most things, including money. So, expand your horizons and talk to new people, read books, articles, or magazines on financial approaches, and explore different cultural practices. The world is a big place, and the collective wisdom of humanity is vast. So, expose yourself to new ideas, challenge your old beliefs, and broaden your understanding of what is possible.
- **Experiment:** When you've identified the habits and beliefs you want to change, take small steps. Start with one new habit or practice and try to commit to it for a week.[21] Whether you're practicing gratitude, looking for positive role models, or using a jar to save, keep in mind that it's all about progress, not perfection. See how this new habit feels and adjust as needed.

By developing a positive relationship with money and embracing an abundance mindset, you can create a financial future that aligns with your values and goals. So, go ahead, explore your money mindset, challenge your beliefs, and start on the path toward a healthier and happier financial life.

Reflection Questions

- How does money mindset affect financial success?
- How can I rewire my beliefs about money?

Exercise – Changing Your Money Mindset

1. **Reflection on Current Money Mindset** – Take a few minutes to jot down your initial thoughts and feelings about money. Be honest with yourself! Do you view money as limited and hard to come by? Do you feel anxious or stressed when thinking about money? These initial thoughts will serve as a baseline for your mindset transformation.
2. **Exploring Abundance Mentality** – Abundance is a way of thinking that focuses on opportunities, possibilities, and the belief that there is enough for everyone. An abundance mindset has *the potential* to positively impact your relationship with money, such as increased creativity and openness to new financial opportunities.
3. **Abundance Affirmations** – Create a list of positive affirmations related to money and abundance. Affirmations can include statements like:
    - "I attract financial opportunities into my life."
    - "There is always enough to meet my needs and desires."
    - "I am open to receiving abundance in all forms."

    Choose one affirmation that resonates with you the most. Write it down on a separate piece of paper and spend a moment reflecting on the meaning behind it.

4. **Visualization Exercise** – Close your eyes, take a few deep breaths, and imagine yourself living with an abundance of financial resources. Visualize the details – the places you go, the things you do, and the experiences you have. Feel the positive emotions associated with financial freedom.
5. **Mindset Commitment** – Return to your affirmation and the initial thoughts you wrote down in Step 1. Reflect on how you can replace scarcity-oriented thoughts with the abundance affirmation you've chosen. Commit to practicing this shift in mindset over the next week.
6. **Journal** – Write about your experiences with your chosen affirmation over the next week (and beyond if you'd like). Reflect on any changes in your thoughts, feelings, or behaviors related to money.

Changing your mindset takes time and consistent effort. Be patient with yourself as you work toward embracing a more positive and abundant perspective on money.

Putting It All Together

Through self-reflection, challenging limiting beliefs, adopting new perspectives, and experimenting with new habits, it is possible to change your money mindset. By doing so, you can create a healthier and happier financial life that aligns with your values and goals. Nurturing your mindset is important, especially when learning how to make money, but we'll talk more about this in the next chapter.

CHAPTER 3

MAKING MONEY

Financial independence is something nearly everyone strives for in life. Fortunately, there are now more options than ever before to make money from home or start a side hustle, regardless of your age. There are three important questions you need to ask yourself:
1. Why do you want a job?
2. What kind of job do you want?
3. How much time do you have to work?

Getting your first job can be exciting and liberating. After all, it's a way to earn money and gain experience that will look good on your resumé for future job applications. Getting a job is a big responsibility, so consider what motivates you to work. Are you working because you want to develop healthy financial habits? Do you want to make your resumé more attractive to future employers? Or do you want to keep busy during your vacation? If you answered "yes" to any of these questions, you are likely intrinsically motivated, which is a good thing. Intrinsic motivation is when you do something because you find it enjoyable, interesting, or personally rewarding. It comes from within yourself, and you engage in an activity simply because you like doing it, not because you are looking for any external rewards or benefits. If you are not intrinsically motivated, chances are you won't learn much from that part-time job you're applying for.[22] That's fine, too; you've got time to figure out what drives you.

Finding the right balance for a part-time job as a young adult can be tricky, and there's no one-size-fits-all answer. It depends on your other commitments and priorities. Here are some things to consider before making a decision:

- **Your state's labor laws:** Different states have restrictions on working hours for teenagers, especially during the school year. Look up your state's labor laws to make sure you stay within the legal limits.
- **Well-being comes first:** If you're overwhelmed with school, sports, and other activities, adding a job on top of that might be too much.
- **Future goals:** If you're looking to build professional connections or explore potential career paths, a job can be valuable. It offers you a chance to gain employment skills, discover your interests, and even find mentors in fields you're curious about.
- **Buffing your resumé:** A job that provides specialized or unique skills can make you a more attractive candidate in the

future. It might set you apart when applying to colleges or jobs down the road.

Be realistic about your schedule and commitments. It's better to start with fewer hours and gradually increase if you can handle it, rather than over-committing and feeling overwhelmed. Toward the end of high school, I juggled a bunch of academic and extracurricular activities while also working about eight hours a week at a part-time job. It was exhausting, and my grades suffered until I modified my schedule to only work on weekends. It's all about finding the right balance for yourself! In the end, only you know what you can handle. Take the time to think about your priorities and what you're willing to commit to before seeking a job. Take care of yourself, and make choices that align with your long-term goals and happiness.

How to Find Jobs

Finding a job does not have to be a horrible, stressful experience. Yes, it can be tough to find a job (especially if you've never written a resumé or attended an interview), but there are some basic steps every job seeker can take to make the process much smoother. These steps include:

- **Discovering your interests:** Look for jobs that align with your hobbies and passions. Nobody wants to be stuck with a job that kills them with boredom.
- **Google search:** As soon as you figure out which jobs align with your hobbies and interests, look for local businesses that might be hiring. Google and local job boards can be very helpful in this search.
- **Apply to interesting jobs:** Make a list of places you'd like to work and apply directly.
- **Don't let rejection demotivate you:** Not every application will result in an interview or a successful hire. Don't be discouraged if you don't get hired right away. Keep trying. You'll eventually find what you're looking for.

- **Prepare for interviews:** Practice answering common questions. A quick Google search will reveal the most common interview questions used in job interviews. Practice answering these questions with a friend or on your own. The key is to project confidence while you are answering these questions.
- **Dress nicely:** Wear clean and presentable clothes when applying or interviewing. No flip-flops, short shorts, ripped jeans, or beachwear. If you're unsure what to wear, err on the side of caution and go for a smart-casual look.
- **Show confidence:** During the interview, be confident, maintain eye contact, and show enthusiasm.[23] How you interact with the interviewer will play a big part in the success of your interview.
- **Follow up:** Send a thank-you message or call after an interview to express your interest.

Remember, finding your first job may take time, but stay persistent, and the right opportunity will come along. Never put your safety at risk for a few dollars by working in a dodgy establishment or any place that ignores safe labor practices and laws.

Different Ways to Earn Money at Any Age

While making money is essential, balancing your work endeavors with your studies, hobbies, and social life is equally important. Always prioritize your well-being and ensure your money-making activities don't hinder your personal growth and development. With determination, resourcefulness, and responsible financial management, you can successfully earn money and gain valuable experiences that will benefit you in the long run. With that being said, here are some ways young adults can make money:

- **Freelance:** If you have skills in areas like graphic design, writing, programming, or video editing, you can offer your services on freelance platforms like Fiverr, Upwork, or Freelancer. Create a profile showcasing your expertise and start bidding on projects that match your abilities. As you complete tasks successfully, you'll build a reputation and attract more clients, enabling you to earn money from your talents.

- **Become a tutor:** Utilize your knowledge in subjects you excel at to become a tutor. Advertise your tutoring services at school or in your community, or use online tutoring platforms to connect with students who need help with their studies. Tutoring can be a rewarding way to make money while helping others succeed academically.
- **Take surveys:** Many companies conduct market research and are willing to pay for people's opinions. Sign up for reputable survey websites or apps that offer paid surveys. While the earnings from each survey may not be substantial, participating in multiple surveys can add up over time, providing you with some extra cash.
- **Work part-time at a restaurant:** Consider getting a part-time job at a local restaurant, cafe, or fast-food chain. This experience will not only help you earn money but also teach you valuable customer service and teamwork skills.[24]
- **Provide lawn and landscaping services:** Take advantage of your physical abilities and offer lawn care and landscaping services to your neighbors or local community. Mowing lawns, weeding gardens, and maintaining outdoor spaces can be profitable ventures, especially during the warmer months.
- **Work as a babysitter/pet sitter:** Babysitting is a classic way for teens to make money. Advertise your babysitting services in your neighborhood or ask family and friends if they need a responsible and trustworthy babysitter/pet sitter. Taking care of children or pets can be a fun and rewarding way to earn money during your free time.[25]
- **Become a lifeguard:** If you're a strong swimmer and have completed lifeguard training and certification, consider working

as a lifeguard during the summer season. Many pools, beaches, and water parks hire lifeguards to ensure the safety of visitors.
- **Sell stuff online:** Declutter your room and sell items you no longer need on online marketplaces like eBay, Facebook Marketplace, or Craigslist. Additionally, you can set up a small online store to sell new or used products like clothes, accessories, or electronics.[26]
- **Invest:** If you have some savings, explore investment options that generate passive income. While investing always carries some risk, you can consider options like opening a high-interest savings account, investing in dividend-paying stocks, or exploring peer-to-peer lending platforms. Investment income allows your money to grow over time, even while you're not actively working.

EXERCISE – MONEY-MAKING: FROM IDEAS TO INCOME

The objective of this exercise is to help you develop a proactive and entrepreneurial mindset toward making money. In this exercise, you will explore creative ideas, assess their feasibility, and develop an action plan to turn your ideas into income-generating opportunities.

Duration: This can be completed over the course of a week, with daily tasks and reflections.

Day 1: Idea Generation
- Brainstorm a list of at least 10 potential money-making ideas. These ideas could range from selling products or services, freelancing, starting a small business, or leveraging your skills and talents.
- No idea is too small or too big at this point. The goal is to think creatively and explore all possibilities.

Day 2: Feasibility Assessment
- Select your top three ideas generated on Day 1.
- For each selected idea, conduct some basic research to see if it's doable. Research might involve understanding your potential

customer, competitors (others offering the same product or service), potential costs to start up, and initial steps required.

Day 3: Skills and Resources
- Evaluate your skills, talents, and resources that could be utilized for each of the three selected ideas.
- How can your existing abilities be leveraged to kick-start your money-making venture without significant upfront investment?

Day 4: Value Proposition
- Of your top three, what kind of value does each idea provide to your potential customer? Write down how your product or service solves a problem or fulfills a need.

Day 5: Action Plan
- Choose the most promising idea from your top three.
- Outline a detailed action plan for your chosen idea. This plan should include specific steps, a timeline, and initial goals. If you need help with this from a friend, mentor, or parent/guardian, then ask!

Day 6: Budgeting and Pricing
- Estimate costs involved in launching your money-making venture and determine how much you need to charge to cover expenses and make a profit.
- Regarding what you're charging your customer, are they paying you once? Are they paying you for a subscription (like how Spotify is a monthly subscription)? Are they paying you more than once for any reason?

Day 7: Pitch and Reflection
- Create a pitch for your money-making idea. This could be a short presentation or an elevator pitch explaining your product or service, its benefits, and its target audience.
- Reflect on the entire process. What did you learn about generating income? What challenges did you encounter? What adjustments would you make to your idea or plan based on your reflections?

Reflection Questions

- What jobs can I get as a high school or college student?
- How can I make money online?

Putting it All Together

Making money is key to achieving financial independence. However, staying motivated and finding the right balance between work and other commitments is just as important. Fortunately, there are many ways you can earn an income and lots of places to store it, and that's exactly what we'll cover in the next chapter.

CHAPTER 4

WHERE TO STORE YOUR MONEY

Banking can be overwhelming for young adults who haven't ever had to handle money before. Understanding the difference between debit and credit cards, learning how to manage a budget, and even selecting the best checking account can all seem intimidating. But with a few basic tips and tricks, anyone can develop a healthy relationship with their bank and gain control of their finances.

A bank is a financial institution that accepts deposits and lends money if we meet certain criteria.[27] Even though there are alternatives available, having a bank account and bank card are often more convenient and secure.

Security

Storing your money in a piggy bank may have worked fine when you were younger, but that option isn't the safest. It's easy to pilfer from someone's stash, and burglars know where people tend to hide their money. Keeping a large stash of money at home inevitably attracts unwanted attention, but there's another risk.

Some unforeseen event, be it a natural disaster or accident, could destroy that piggy bank and all the money inside. Homeowner's insurance will only cover a limited amount of cash, so you could be out of luck if you had a lot saved. Keeping all your money at home isn't safe, even if you bury it in the backyard. That's because the container could corrode over time, or, worse still, your money could start decomposing. Yes, money can decompose. Here's a fun fact: The $10 bill has an average lifespan of five years.[28]

Then there's the option of keeping all your cash on a prepaid debit card. You won't need a bank account if you have one of those, right? That's not quite the case. Bank accounts are more secure than prepaid debit cards for a very good reason. Prepaid cards are subject to fewer controls than debit cards issued by banks.[29] While a prepaid debit card is more convenient than cash, it can still be stolen or lost.

A bank is one of the most secure places you can keep your money. As long as the bank is legitimate and has Federal Deposit Insurance Corporation (FDIC) insurance or National Credit Union Association insurance, the money you deposit is protected up to $250,000.[30]

Convenience

A bank account allows us to access our money from anywhere. It could be the ATM, the corner grocery store, or across town, but there's no shortage of ways to access and use your money. A checking account also simplifies the process of paying bills.

How to Choose a Bank

Choosing a bank can be a tricky task, but with a little know-how, you'll be able to choose a reputable bank with ease. It's true that big-name banks can fail, but if they had FDIC insurance, your money would be protected. Some banks may serve your needs better than others, so here's what to look for when deciding where to open your bank account.

Bank Legitimacy and Reputation

You'll want to make sure the bank you are using (or want to use) is legit. Going with large, widely-known banks is usually a safe bet. If you want to be extra safe, go to the FDIC's website and use the search tool to search for the bank.

Finding a bank with a good reputation is a different story. Many well-known banks have made headlines for misdeeds such as bribing officials or manipulating interest rates. So, it is vital that you do your research on a bank's reputation before committing to it. You need to feel comfortable with the bank you choose.

Online Only vs. Brick-and-Mortar Banks

Another big decision when it comes to banks is choosing between an online-only or a physical bank. Most banks have a strong online presence, even if they started as brick-and-mortar institutions. This means features like online bill pay, mobile check deposits, and apps that allow you to bank anytime, anywhere, should be standard features.

But what's the big difference between an old-school walk-in bank and an online one? The difference boils down to this: fees and interest rates. Online-only banks have lower overhead costs because they don't have a physical location. That means no building lease, maintenance, or other fees to pay. These savings get passed on to consumers, and there are usually no pesky monthly maintenance fees or minimum balance requirements with online-only banks. The bonus is that these banks can afford to give us higher interest rates on savings accounts and certificates of deposit. So, essentially, we're getting a bit more value for our money.

But... traditional banks sometimes offer the same sweet deals as online-only banks. They give you low fees and high rates, but they also give you the option to actually sit down and chat with a real-life banker. So, if face-to-face interaction is your thing, don't write off regular banks just yet. Traditional banks might surprise you with low-fee accounts, so it's worth checking them out too.

What is worth considering is the kind of banking experience you're after. Not nearly enough people consider this point before choosing their bank, and it can make a huge difference in your financial well-being. Ask yourself:

- Do you prefer talking to people, or do you prefer to let the bank's AI work its magic?
- Are you channeling that old-school spirit by writing checks, or do you like to pay your bills online?

If you regularly make deposits, be aware that this can be a hassle at some online banks. They will typically require you to use a special ATM, money order, or some other intermediary that may not be convenient.

Bank Size and Location

If you've got your heart set on opening an account with a bank that has a physical location, you'll need to consider how convenient it will be for you. Most people want a bank that's relatively close to where they live, work, or go to school. It just makes it easier to make deposits and sort out money-related matters without having to go too far out of your way. If you find yourself traveling a lot, do some digging to find out which banks will give you access to your cash when you're out of town. The last thing you want is to be stranded without access to your own money. It's a horrible feeling.

There are perks to going with the online-only banks, too! Usually, these banks have a network of ATMs across the country that customers can use without paying any fees. In fact, some online-only banks may reimburse you for a certain number of out-of-network ATM fees per month.

Banking Fees

Some banks remain free to use for as long as you can keep your account balance positive. Other banks slap their customers with fees for every transaction. Small fees can add up quickly over time and eat into your hard-earned savings, so you'll need to look at the bank's fee schedule to make sure they won't fleece you. Even if you sign up with a bank that advertises a lifetime of "free checking," rest assured there are fees hidden somewhere. You may have to pay fees if your balance drops below a certain threshold, for not depositing a check directly into your account, overdrawing the account, requesting paper statements, using the ATM, or even closing your account, so keep an eye out for those annoying hidden fees.

DIFFERENT TYPES OF BANK ACCOUNTS

After selecting a bank, you'll be faced with another tough-ish decision. Which account should you open? Not every type of bank account is the same, and some may penalize you for withdrawing money at the wrong time. A basic checking or savings account are both great places to start and are options offered at all banks.[31] Let's take a closer look at the different types of accounts banks offer.

Checking Account

This is a basic bank account into which you can deposit your paycheck. This account type allows you to pay bills and generally gives you easy access to your money. Checking accounts come with a debit card, so there's no need to have cash on you. When swiping your card to pay, keep in mind that some purchases may take a few days to process. It depends on the vendor. The cool thing is that a checking account can make paying bills much easier. These accounts typically give the option to set up automatic bill pay, so you'll never miss a payment. Here's what to look out for in a checking account:
- Online banking, either through an app or the bank's website

- Accepts direct deposits
- No maintenance cost or minimum balance required

If you are considering switching to a checking account, there are a few things to watch out for. Big banks and some credit unions sure love their fees, so you'll need to do your research carefully before making the switch. Here are some of the most common fees to look out for on a checking account:

- **Overdraft fee:** With a checking account, it's possible to spend more than what you have in your account, causing your bank balance to go into the negative. That's what the banks call "overdrafting" and can come with a steep charge if you're not careful.
- **Bounced check fee:** When working with old-school paper checks, remember that there's a lag between the day the check is written and the day it gets cashed. While there's technically no expiration date on checks, most banks won't cash checks older than six months. So, when you write a check, take care not to accidentally spend that money; otherwise, your bank could slap you with a fee for processing a returned (bounced) check.
- **Monthly maintenance fees:** This is another avenue where banks make a ton of easy cash. But is the cost justified? Even if your account only costs six dollars a month, that turns into $72 a year that you could have used for other purposes.

Savings Account

A checking account and savings account generally go great together, just like Shrek and Donkey, Rick and Morty, or SpongeBob and Patrick. Checking accounts give us a convenient way to spend our money, while savings accounts give us a way to save. These accounts are great if you plan on having access to emergency funds. For example, if you know your car is due for maintenance or if you want to upgrade your computer to a sweet gaming rig, you'll want to budget for these expenses and set the money aside in a savings account. If you keep the cash in your checking account, you might accidentally spend it. Keep in mind that a savings account won't make you rich. It's a tool we can use to budget better and hone our skills to save money. Here's what to look for in a savings account:

- Competitive interest rate (interest rates on savings accounts are notoriously low, but it's better than nothing).
- Online banking features (this includes the ability to accept transfers from your checking account).
- No maintenance fee every month

Note: the interest earned on a savings account is considered taxable income, so you'll need to be on top of your taxes (don't worry, we'll cover taxes in Chapter 10). Also, keep in mind that some banks may require you to maintain a minimum balance in your account, and there might be limits to the number of transfers and withdrawals you make every month.

Money Market Account

These are kind of like a cross between a checking account and a savings account. Like a checking account, the money market account may come with a debit card, but not all banks offer this feature as standard. Like with a savings account, a money market account earns you interest. The interest isn't much, but it's usually a smidgen more than what you'd earn with a regular savings account. This type of bank account is great for stashing your emergency funds. Here's what you need to watch out for in a money market account:

- Limits on the number of monthly transfers and withdrawals.
- A minimum balance may be applicable to keep the account open and for maintenance. Fees may become applicable if the amount in the account drops below the minimum balance.
- Interest earned is minimal, but it is taxable.

CREDIT CARDS VS. DEBIT CARDS

Using a credit or debit card can be very helpful in learning important money lessons. Research shows that more and more kids are learning these lessons early on, as 17% of people between the ages of 8 and 14 have a credit card.[32]

Debit cards don't let you rack up debt, which is a good thing, whereas credit cards can actually help you build credit and offer better protections. You'll need to take a look at the features, pros, and cons of each type to find the best fit for you. If you're itching to get your own credit card and you're under 18 and unemployed, you're out of luck. It's not as simple as just applying and getting approved. The law actually requires proof of income (your allowance doesn't count) from ages 18 to 21 to show that you can handle the charges. If you are under 18, a parent or guardian can add you as an authorized user on one of their accounts. This means you can use the card and have your activity reported on your credit report. However, keep in mind that your parent or guardian will still be responsible for the balance. It is a privilege that should not be misused.

If you're leaning more toward a debit card, you might be surprised to learn that some banks actually offer them to kids as young as 8, as long as a parent or guardian is an account co-owner. Typically, you'll find checking accounts open to minors in the age range of 13 to 17. So getting your hands on a debit card may prove easier than a credit card.

Let's talk about why getting a credit card might be a good idea for you. First off, adding a credit card to your name can help you build a credit history, which will come in handy when you need to borrow money for a car or a mortgage in the future. Having a good credit score also makes it easier to get approved for credit and borrow at favorable interest rates. It can even save you the trouble of having to get a cosigner (someone legally obligated to pay back your debt if you don't), which could impact their credit score.

Credit cards also provide better protection against fraud compared to debit cards. If your card gets lost or stolen and someone goes on a shopping spree, the law limits your liability. Some issuers even offer additional benefits that won't cost you anything as a cardholder. On top of that, credit cards often come with cool features like cash-back rewards. You can save money or start a savings account with the cash back you earn.

Now, let's talk about the downsides of credit cards. The temptation to overspend can be strong, no matter what age you are. This can lead to debt accumulating and your finances being negatively impacted. A credit card is a privilege, not a golden ticket to live beyond your means and splurge on purchasing cheats for favorite video game. But with some education and responsible use, you can avoid getting into trouble with credit card debt.

Of course, there are drawbacks to debit cards too. They don't offer the same level of fraud protection as credit cards, so if your card is lost or stolen, you could be held responsible for fraudulent charges. Big yikes. Also, using a debit card won't help you build or access credit. Despite these drawbacks, debit cards are still way safer than keeping your money in a piggy bank.

When choosing a credit card, make sure to check the basics, like the annual percentage rate (APR), any fees, and the card benefits.

Keeping Money in Your Accounts

Now that we've gained a better understanding of bank accounts, let's explore the various ways you can deposit money. Whether you're looking to deposit funds into your own account or someone else's, there are a few options available to you.

- **Depositing cash in person:** If you have cash on hand, you can deposit it by visiting the bank that holds the account. However, some banks may have restrictions on cash deposits made into an account that doesn't bear your name. These restrictions are in place to prevent money laundering and fraud since cash transactions are difficult to trace.
- **Electronic transfer:** Transferring money into a bank account has become quite convenient with services like Cash App, PayPal, Venmo, Zelle, and similar platforms. However, it's important to exercise caution when using these services, as payments made are often irreversible. Because these apps don't have the same consumer protection as bank accounts, once you receive money in one of these apps, move it to your bank account as soon as possible.
- **Wire transfer:** For a wire transfer, you'll need three essential pieces of information: the recipient's name, account number, and routing number. Wire transfers are a suitable option when you need to send large amounts of money to an account. Most banks do not impose limits on wire transfers, and domestic transfers are processed quickly. However, it's worth noting that wire transfers can be costly.
- **Personal check:** Paper checks can be deposited into your own account or someone else's. Money deposited through checks can be traced by financial institutions, making them a safer option compared to cash. However, be aware that funds from a

check may not be immediately available. Depending on the bank, it may take hours or even days for a check to clear.
- **Cashier's check:** Also known as a bank check, this type of check can be obtained directly from a bank. Cashier's checks eliminate the risk of bouncing and often clear faster than personal checks.
- **Money order:** Similar to checks, money orders are paper documents that are used to move money into accounts but are not tied to a specified bank account. Money orders can be purchased at banks, credit unions, post offices, and some retailers. Just like a check, there is a cost to processing the money order, but it is relatively inexpensive.

As you can see, there are a few different ways we can move money around, so it's best to do your research beforehand and use the methods that work best for you.

REFLECTION QUESTIONS

- What is a checking account? How is this different from a savings account?
- How can I open a checking account?

EXERCISE (REVIEW) – THE CREDIT CRUNCH

Scenario 1 – The Casual Shopper

Meet Sarah, 18, who recently got her first credit card with a $500 limit. She's excited about the newfound financial freedom and decides to go shopping. She buys a new phone for $300, clothes for $150, and goes out to eat with friends, spending an additional $50. At the end of the month, she receives her credit card statement with an interest rate of 18% APR (Annual Percentage Rate).

Transaction Details:

- Phone: $300

- Clothes: $150
- Dining: $50

Interest Rate: 18% APR

Sarah has a choice to make regarding her payment:

Choice 1 - Minimum Payment: The credit card company requires Sarah to pay a minimum of 2% of the outstanding balance or $25, whichever is higher.

Choice 2 - Full Payment: Sarah decides to pay off the entire balance.

Calculations:

- Total Spent: $300 + $150 + $50 = $500

Choice 1 - Minimum Payment:

- Minimum Payment = 2% of $500 = $10
- Remaining Balance = $500 - $10 = $490
- Interest for the month = (18% / 12) * $490 = $7.75
- Total Amount Due = $10 (Minimum Payment) + $7.75 (Interest) = $17.75

Impact: If Sarah chooses the minimum payment option, she'll only pay $17.75 this month, but the remaining balance of $490 will continue to accumulate interest. Over time, this can lead to a significant amount of debt.

Choice 2 - Full Payment:

- Total Amount Due = $500 (Total Spent) + $0 (Interest) = $500

Impact: If Sarah chooses the full payment option, she'll pay off her entire balance and avoid paying any interest. This choice helps her maintain good credit and financial health.

Scenario 2 – Buying the Essentials

Mark is a college senior with a credit limit of $2,000. He uses his card primarily for essentials. This month, he purchased a plane ticket for $800 to visit his family, bought groceries for $150, and paid his monthly subscription services totaling $30. He also bought a textbook from his university for $300. The credit card has an interest rate of 15% APR.

Transaction Details:

- Plane Ticket: $800
- Groceries: $150
- Subscriptions: $30
- Textbook Loan: $300

Interest Rate: 15% APR

Mark, too, has two payment choices:

Choice 1 - Minimum Payment: The credit card company's minimum payment is 2% of the outstanding balance or $30, whichever is higher.

Choice 2 - Payment of Choice: Mark decides to pay off $500 this month.

Calculations:

- Total Spent: $800 + $150 + $30 + $300 = $1,280

Choice 1 - Minimum Payment:

- Minimum Payment = 2% of $1,280 = $25.60
- Remaining Balance = $1,280 - $25.60 = $1,254.40
- Interest for the month = (15% / 12) * $1,254.40 = $15.68
- Total Amount Due = $25.60 (Minimum Payment) + $15.68 (Interest) = $41.28

Impact: If Mark opts for the minimum payment, he'll pay $41.28, and a significant portion will go toward interest. The remaining balance will continue to accrue interest.

Choice 2 - Payment of Choice:

- Remaining Balance = $1,280 - $500 = $780
- Interest for the month = (15% / 12) * $780 = $9.75
- Total Amount Due = $500 (Payment) + $9.75 (Interest) = $509.75

Impact: By choosing to pay off $500, Mark reduces his balance significantly and minimizes the interest he'll have to pay. This helps him save money and maintain control over his finances.

Bottom line: In both scenarios, it's evident that responsible credit card use, which includes paying off the balance in full whenever possible, can lead to better financial outcomes and less debt accumulation.

PUTTING IT ALL TOGETHER

There's a lot of information about money out there that can be hard to digest. However, if you understand the importance of having a bank account, know what to look for in different types of accounts, and know the difference between a credit and debit card, you are well on your way to mastering your finances. Now that you have the fundamentals down pat, it's time to teach yourself an essential skill that will change your finance game forever. Yes, I'm talking about budgeting basics, but more on that in the next chapter.

CHAPTER 5

BUDGETING BASICS

Budgeting is a great way to get a handle on your finances and maximize your savings. Sadly, when it comes to decisions that make good financial sense, people usually forget about budgeting. A recent survey found that nearly 73% of Americans don't stick to a budget.[33] So many people choose to eyeball their expenses and income, instead of getting a clearer picture of what's going on with their money. So, what exactly is a budget? Simply put, it's a plan for how you will spend your money. Without a good plan, it's all too easy to go into the kind of debt that takes over your life.

Teaching yourself budgeting skills is not difficult. First, we need to understand that budgeting is a balancing act, kind of like playing on a seesaw. You'll want to strike a balance between the four main areas of a monthly budget, which will help you make smarter money choices in the future. The main areas of budgeting that are vital to get a handle on are:

- **Income:** Your income is the money you earn, whether it be from a part-time job pet-sitting for your neighbors, an allowance from your parents, or a paid summer internship. List all your sources of income so you'll know what your total income is for the month.
- **Expenses:** Here is where most budgeting falls flat. Many people don't realize they have to split their expenses into two categories, i.e., fixed and variable expenses. Fixed expenses are those expenses that stay the same every month, such as a gym membership, rent, or a cellphone plan. Variable expenses differ from month to month and include things like dining out, travel, gas, entertainment, or that impulsive shopping spree.[34] As a result, these expenses can easily break our budgets. We can't do much about fixed expenses, but we can control how we spend our money on variable expenses.
- **Saving and investing:** Spoiler alert – if you're old enough to make money, you're also old enough to learn about investing and saving. Budgeting will help you see how much money you have left over to save every month. That's money that can be stashed into a savings account for a rainy day. Set a monthly goal for saving and make it part of your budget. The savings will add up pretty quickly if you manage to stick to your plan.
- **Debt:** If you have any debts (like a credit card or student loan), it is crucial to include the payments in your budget. Debt can spread faster than the latest celebrity gossip, so always make a point of budgeting to pay down any money you may owe.

How to Start Budgeting

Budgeting doesn't have to be intimidating. The secret to being successful is to be consistent with your budget. Learning how to do a zero-based budget is super easy! Having a zero-based budget does not mean your bank account is empty, it simply means that if we deduct our expenses from our income, the total would be zero.[35]

So if you make $1,000 a month, everything you spent, gave, or saved should add up to $1,000. That means every dollar earned has a purpose, and nothing is wasted on fancy coffees or bargain bin deals. So, what could a zero-based budget look like? Let's use the $1,000 income mentioned earlier as an example. To create a zero-based budget, start by listing all your expenses and assigning your income to different categories.

- **Fixed expenses:** These expenses are fixed, like your rent and utilities. Let's say your total fixed expenses amount to $500.
- **Variable expenses:** These expenses fluctuate from month to month, like groceries and clothing. Let's say your total variable expenses amount to $300.
- **Financial goals:** These are savings or investments you want to make to achieve your financial objectives. Let's say you want to save $200 per month.
- **Debt:** If you have any debt to pay off (credit cards, student loans, or a loan from your parents), you'll need to include it in your budget. In this example, we don't have debt, so we don't need to allocate anything toward repayments.
- **Miscellaneous:** This category can include unexpected expenses or items that don't fit into the other categories (e.g., savings or charitable giving). Let's allocate $0 for this category to maintain a balanced budget.

Now, if you add up your expenses, you'll see that your expenses and income match perfectly. By allocating your income to specific categories, you've ensured that every dollar you earn has a purpose and that your total expenses match your income. In a zero-based budget, you prioritize your spending and avoid overspending since you have a clear plan for your money.

Did you know that the average Gen Z-er spends about $2,600 every year?[36] That's a lot of cash. A zero-based budget is a great place to start taking control of your financial future, and it can help you avoid wasteful expenditures. I appreciate that we all have different tastes, wants, and needs, so each person's budget will be different. That being said, there are some things we need to be careful of, otherwise, we could find ourselves eating through our money way too quickly.

- **Takeout and fancy coffee:** Find yourself buying Wendy's or Starbucks every day? While that Mocha Cookie Crumble Frappuccino is tasty, the costs will soon add up. Do yourself a favor and calculate all the money you've spent on takeout and fancy coffee over the last two weeks. That number is not what you expected, eh?
- **Being trendy:** It's normal for young people to take pride in their style. However, fast fashion comes with a price. Not only do those super trendy outfits fall out of fashion (and apart) quite quickly, but the manufacturing process in fast fashion is a big environmental no-no. That's because fashion production is responsible for 10% of global carbon emissions.[37] The sad thing is that most of these garments end up in the dump anyway. Our

planet is paying a hefty price for our wasteful ways, so invest in quality clothing before falling victim to a fast fad. Quality never goes out of style, either.
- **Prom:** Getting ready for that big dance at school can be expensive! Renting a tux, getting that perfect dress, and organizing a sweet limo ride are the standard ingredients for a school dance. With college or major life decisions right around the corner, getting into a mountain of debt to be boujee for one night might not be worth it.
- **Entertainment:** Gaming consoles and concert tickets are black holes that can drain every last dime from your account if you're not careful. There's nothing wrong with having fun and enjoying yourself with the things you love, but at $60 a pop for a game, it can become pricey.

Exercise - Setting SMART Savings Goals

There are other money-sapping pitfalls we need to be careful of, but most of them can be avoided by setting goals. It's great to have goals, but sometimes they can be vague, making it hard to know when you achieve them. That's where SMART goals come in! Let's see how it works with an example of saving money:
- **Specific (S):** The first step is to make your goal specific. Ask yourself, what are you saving for? Maybe one of your goals is to have some emergency money.
- **Measurable (M):** Next, make your goal measurable. How much money do you want to save? Let's say you want to save $400.
- **Attainable (A):** Is this goal realistic and doable for you? Take a moment to think about whether you can realistically achieve it. Maybe you can earn some extra money or find ways to spend less.
- **Relevant (R):** Is this goal worth saving for? Think about why it's important to you. Saving for unexpected costs, like emergencies, is definitely worth it.

- **Timebound (T):** Lastly, set a timeframe for when you want to achieve your goal. Let's say you want to reach your savings goal in 3 months, which is about 12 weeks.

By making your goal SMART, you've made it clearer and easier to track your progress. Now, you know exactly what you're saving for, how much you want to save, and when you want to reach your goal. It helps you stay focused and motivated! The budgeting worksheet below will help you keep track of your income, expenses, and savings goals.

	Sources and amounts	Total
Income	Allowance: $xx	Add your totals together to find out how much income you have every month.
	Job: $xx	
	Other: $xx	
Expenses (List all your expenses, both fixed and variable.)	Rent: $xx	Add your totals together to find out how much you are spending every month.
	Cellphone: $xx	
	Transportation: $xx	
	Other fixed expenses: $xx	
	Groceries and personal care: $xx	
	Other variable expenses: $xx	
Savings (Write your SMART savings goal down.)	The amount you want to save: $xxx	Add your savings totals together to calculate how much you should be saving each month.
Remaining balance		Calculate your remaining balance by subtracting your total expenses from your total income.

By using this budgeting worksheet, you can keep track of your income, expenses, and savings goals. It will help you understand where your money is going and how much you can save. Be sure to review and update the worksheet regularly, as your income and expenses may change.

Reflection Questions

- How do you start a budget?
- What are the five key pieces to setting a SMART savings goal?

Putting it All Together

Budgeting has many benefits tied to it. When you master the art of sticking to your budget, you'll be able to save and avoid unnecessary debt. Setting SMART savings goals can help you take control of your finances and make wise money choices, which are the basics of being responsible with money. In the next chapter, we'll take a closer look at how to use credit cards responsibly so you don't have to blow your budget on debt repayment!

CHAPTER 6

MANAGING CREDIT

Building a good credit score at any age can be challenging, but it's not impossible. A credit score is a three-digit number that shows how likely people are to pay their bills on time.[38] The number ranges from 300–850, it's kind of like a GPA but for money management. The higher the score, the better! Banks and credit card companies use this score to determine if you are eligible for credit.

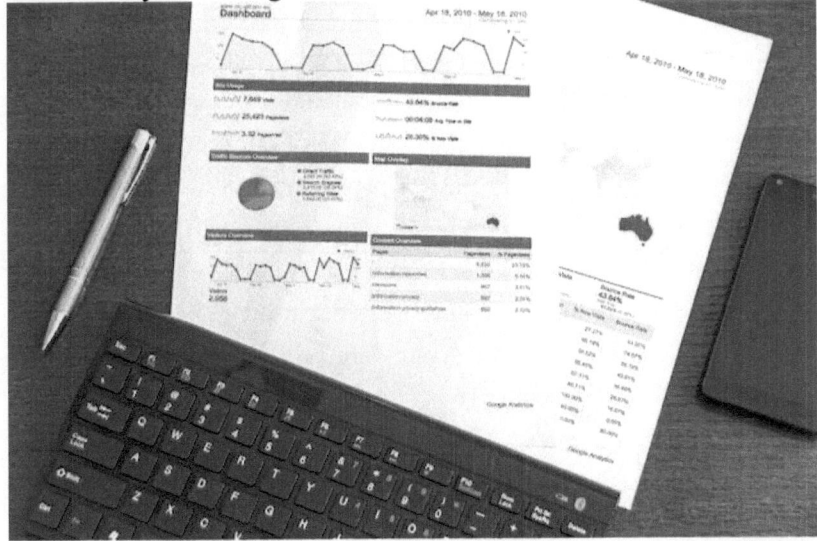

But where does a credit score come from? There are three big credit bureaus in the United States.[39] They are TransUnion, Equifax, and Experian. The job of these bureaus is to analyze credit information and pass it along to lenders (like banks and credit card companies) to help them make informed decisions on loans. The most widely used credit score is FICO, and here's what those numbers mean:

- **Poor credit score:** 300–579
- **Fair:** 580–669
- **Good:** 670–739
- **Very good:** 740–799
- **Exceptional:** 800 and upwards

These ranges are important, as it is incredibly difficult to get a loan or other forms of credit with a low FICO score. Just like a GPA determines which colleges will accept you, your credit score will determine how easily you'll be able to borrow money and at what rates. Unlike a GPA, it's always possible to improve your credit score, but you'll need to know how credit scores work first. We can think of a credit report as a history of our financial activity. It shows us all the money we've borrowed and how good we were at paying it back. These details are then used to create a credit score. There are five things that contribute to this score, including:

1. **Payment history:** Late payments will lower your credit score, while timely payments can keep it steady or even give it a little boost. Payment history makes up 35% of our credit score, so we really can't ignore debt and skip payments if we want a good credit record.
2. **Credit utilization:** This is how much debt versus credit you have. For example, if you have a credit card with a limit of $5,000 and your current balance (your debt on the card) is $500, then your credit utilization is 10%.[40] A good rule of thumb is to keep your credit utilization under 30% so you won't find yourself in a situation where you are drowning in debt.
3. **Credit history:** This is the average total length of each credit account you've opened. Keeping credit in good standing is easy: All you need to do is successfully pay off your debts. Credit history makes up 15% of your final credit score.

4. **Credit mix:** You can have a mix of different types of credit, such as credit cards and loans. It's a good idea to have a mix of debt types, but you don't need one of every kind. Your credit mix only makes up 10% of your final credit score, so don't go crazy here.
5. **New credit:** This is any new debt that has been added to your credit report in the last six months. It's a good idea to establish additional credit but be careful of applying for too many new accounts in a short period of time, as this can hurt your credit score. Be cautious and deliberate when applying for credit, and space out those applications to nullify any negative effect they might have on your credit score. Even though new credit only makes up 10% of your final credit score, it can still have a lasting impact if you're not careful.

DIFFERENT TYPES OF CREDIT

I've mentioned that your credit mix is considered when your credit score is calculated. While this category only makes up a small percentage (10%) of your final credit score, it is good to know what types of credit are lurking in the wild:

- **Credit cards:** In Chapter 4, we discussed credit cards. This is a form of credit that allows you to borrow money from a credit card issuer to make purchases. Credit cards are useful for building a credit history, but they need to be used responsibly to avoid piling up high-interest debt.
- **Mortgages:** These are loans specifically designed for the purchase of homes. When you get a mortgage, the lender will give you the funds needed to buy the property, but you need to make monthly repayments over several years. Usually, mortgages are paid off over 15 to 30 years.
- **Personal loan:** An unsecured loan is a fixed amount of money that you need to repay over a set term with fixed monthly

payments. Personal loan interest rates vary and are frequently influenced by your credit history.
- **Line of credit:** This is a flexible form of borrowing that allows people to access funds. There's a predetermined credit limit, and it works a lot like a credit card, but with one difference. Instead of making purchases, you can withdraw the cash or transfer it directly into your bank account. Interest is usually only charged on the amount used, and as soon as you repay what you've borrowed, the money becomes available again.
- **Payday loans:** These loans are short-term and super expensive to pay back! The loan is usually intended for small amounts and is generally considered a risky form of credit as it can trap borrowers easily in a cycle of debt.

So, how can you make use of the different types of credit to build a healthy credit record as a teen or college student? The good news is that establishing a good credit score is more accessible than most people assume. Taking proactive steps early can lay a strong foundation for a solid financial future. Here are some of the ways young adults can do this:
- **Shared credit cards:** In Chapter 4, I mentioned that parents and guardians can help their kids build their credit score through a shared credit card. This is a practical, hands-on way for you to gain experience managing money while working on your credit score. Keep in mind that missed payments will affect everyone's credit score if you go this route!
- **Shared bank account:** Even though a shared bank account doesn't play a role in a credit report, most places where you'll apply for credit will require you to have a bank account to receive loan deposits. Also, maintaining a minimum balance (usually a few hundred dollars) can help with credit approvals.[41]
- **Federal student loans:** These loans are reported to the major credit bureaus and can help establish a credit history. Private student loans are also reported to credit bureaus, but

they don't have the same benefits as federal student loans. That's because most federal student loans have a fixed interest rate and don't require a credit check, making it that much easier to get started. Student loans can be one of the costliest ways to start a credit history, and missing payments will definitely affect your credit score.

- **A secured credit card**: Think of this as an introduction to other forms of credit. Many secured credit cards link to your bank account to confirm there's enough money to use the cards, and regular monthly statements give you enough time to make payments on time. Take good care of your secured credit card by using it responsibly and paying it on time, and you'll eventually qualify for an unsecured credit card that has a much higher limit and different types of loans. *Note*: I got started late building my credit score. And I actually used one of these in my mid-twenties. It had a $500 limit, and it helped get my credit score where it needed to be while teaching me a valuable lesson about credit and spending.

Reflection Questions

- How does a credit card differ from a debit card?
- How can I establish good credit ASAP?

Exercise (Review) – Building Credit

Scenario 1 – Good Way to Build Credit

Meet Ha-joon, an 18-year-old community college student, eager to start building his credit responsibly. He decides to apply for a secured credit card. He does his research and chooses a card with a low annual fee and reasonable interest rates. He understands that a secured credit card requires him to make a security deposit, which becomes his credit limit. This way, he can't spend beyond his means.

Steps taken:
1. **Limited Usage:** Ha-joon uses the credit card for small, planned purchases, like groceries and textbooks, that he can afford to pay off each month.
2. **Full Payments:** He pays off his credit card balance in full before the due date every month. This helps him avoid paying interest and demonstrates responsible repayment behavior.
3. **Credit Utilization:** He keeps his credit utilization (the ratio of credit used to the credit limit) below 30%, which positively impacts his credit score.
4. **Consistent Payments:** Ha-joon ensures all his bills, including the credit card bill, are paid on time. Payment history is a major factor in calculating credit scores.
5. **Monitoring:** He regularly checks his credit reports to ensure accuracy and detect any fraudulent activity.

Results: Over time, Ha-joon's responsible credit card usage helps him build a positive credit history. His credit score improves, and when he graduates from college, he has a solid credit foundation that opens doors to better financial opportunities.

Scenario 2 – Bad Way to Build Credit

Meet Alex, a 20-year-old who doesn't fully understand the implications of credit card usage. Alex recently received several credit card offers in the mail and is excited about the idea of having access to seemingly free money. They don't realize credit cards come with responsibilities and consequences. Alex applies for multiple credit cards without reading the terms and conditions. Alex uses the credit cards to live beyond their means.

Steps taken:
1. **Maxed Out Cards:** Alex uses all their credit cards to make impulsive purchases, including expensive gadgets, dining out frequently, and even a spontaneous weekend trip.

2. **Minimum Payments:** Alex only pays the minimum amount due on credit card bills, thinking it's sufficient to keep their accounts in good standing.
3. **High Credit Utilization:** Due to excessive spending, Alex's credit utilization skyrockets well beyond 50%, negatively impacting their credit score.
4. **Late Payments:** With so many bills to manage, Alex occasionally misses credit card payments, leading to late fees and a tarnished payment history.
5. **Debt Accumulation:** Over time, the interest on Alex's credit card balances accumulates, leaving Alex in deep debt with no clear plan to pay it off.

Results: Alex's impulsive credit card behavior quickly leads to financial troubles. Their credit score plummets due to high utilization, late payments, and accumulating debt. As a result, Alex faces limited access to loans, higher interest rates, and difficulty renting an apartment in the future. Credit mismanagement takes a toll on Alex's overall financial well-being.

Putting it All Together

Whatever stage of life you're in, equipping yourself to reach your financial goals is vital. It takes credit to build credit, and luckily, there are several ways you can go about this responsibly. Remember to take small steps and thoroughly understand what your credit score means and what you can do to improve it. Now that you know what you can do to get your mitts on credit, the next chapter will be very important as well: dealing with debt.

CHAPTER 7

DEALING WITH DEBT

Debt can be overwhelming and stressful. No matter what debts you are facing, the most important thing is to take action and start developing a plan. Part of becoming financially literate is understanding the ins and outs of good and bad debt. There are different types of debt that you can rack up, and not all debt is bad. But how can you tell the difference between good and bad debt, and how can it impact your finances? Mastering the art of handling money so you don't have to worry about financial troubles later in life is an essential life skill, especially if you'd like to be able to retire as early as possible and never have to worry about money like Oprah.

Good debt can help you increase your income over time and should have a lower interest rate than bad debt. Student loans are often (but not always) a great example of good debt, as you are investing in your future by working toward a degree or credential that will boost your earning potential. It's no secret that college graduates earn more over their lifetimes than people who only hold a high school diploma. In fact, the poverty rate for degree holders tends to be three and a half times lower than for those with high school diplomas.[42] In this context, it is understandable how student loans can be considered good debt.

Bad debt is any debt that can hold you back from financial success.[43] Credit cards are often considered a form of bad debt because they have high interest rates and can accumulate some serious interest. Some credit card companies are like toxic friends. They will offer you an incentive or reward to encourage you to spend more money on your credit card. It might seem like a sweet deal at first, but if you're not careful, you can be trapped in a nasty debt cycle. By following these golden rules, you can prevent yourself from falling into this toxic debt trap in the first place.

- Only borrow what you can pay back.
- Clearly differentiate between your wants and needs (more details in Chapter 2).
- Make a personal budget and stick to it (details on budgeting are in Chapter 5).
- Understand how much debt will cost to repay.
- Never ignore debt, as it could get you into trouble.

EXERCISE – OPTIONS TO GET OUT OF DEBT (AND STAY OUT)

Debt is one of those problems that gets worse if you ignore it. Even though managing debt might feel overwhelming at first, the first step to getting yourself out of trouble is to be real about your situation. You'll need to list exactly how much you owe and to whom if you want to become debt-free successfully. Once you have a clear picture of your financial situation, it becomes easier to devise a plan to pay off debt. Here are three ways you can go about becoming debt-free:

1. **Debt avalanche method:** This approach requires you to pay off high-interest debt first, gradually working your way down to pay off the lowest-interest debt.[44] You'll need to keep up the minimum payments on the other debts that you have to avoid falling into deeper trouble. Any extra money in the budget typically goes toward prioritized debt. While this method is not a speedy way to get out of debt, it can result in you paying less money overall toward debt as you are getting rid of high-interest debt first.

2. **Debt snowball method:** Here, you focus on paying off smaller debts first and then work your way up to the big debts. The interest rate does not matter much here, the size of the debt does.

3. **50/30/20 rule:** This popular guiding principle states that we need to divide our income as follows: 50% toward needs, 30% toward wants, and 20% toward savings or debt repayment.[45] Usually, people try to repay their debt before saving, so if you are using this principle, try to allocate 20% of your income toward debt repayments.

Regardless of the strategy you choose to follow, you'll need to figure out a budget so you can pay down that debt. Budgeting is vital for any financial plan, but these tips can help make that budget stretch and pay down debt even faster.

- **Pay more than the minimum:** Here's something about debt repayment that not enough people are talking about: interest. Debt comes with interest; that's nothing new. But interest can become a cash vacuum, especially if we only make the minimum payment on our debt each month. Whatever is left of the payment (which is usually very little) gets applied to reducing the principal (the amount you borrowed). If you stick to minimum payments, it can take a very long time to make a significant dent in your debt. If you're following the snowball or avalanche method, it's a different story, as minimum payments are part of the plan.

- **Stop going out to eat:** For now, cut down on extra expenses such as eating out and splurging on your favorite fast food snacks. Trust me, those extra few dollars every week add up quickly and can help wipe out your debt quicker! It doesn't mean you have to stick to "boring" foods or never slurp on a satisfying coffee again. Not at all! You can still enjoy good foods and tasty drinks at a fraction of the price by learning how to make them yourself. Who knows? You might discover a hidden talent, and that's always a bonus!

- **Avoid expensive hobbies:** Everyone needs an outlet, but some hobbies can be very expensive. One such hobby is gaming. Gaming systems can be pricey, and games aren't cheap either. Consider leaving expensive hobbies on the back burner while you are sorting your debt out, you can always resumé that hobby when your finances are in better shape.

- **Find free entertainment:** Entertainment is all around us if you know where to look. Best of all, it does not cost a dime or require the internet! Channel your old-school spirit and visit

your local library, try your hand at bird-watching if you live near a park or wooded area, or teach yourself a new skill (such as calligraphy, cooking, or gardening). You'll be surprised how engrossing learning a new skill can be!
- **Use the envelope system:** The envelope system is an effective budgeting method, especially if you prefer a hands-on approach to managing money. It's super easy to set up this system. After you've gone through the steps of creating a budget and allocating funds to each category, you'll need to get your hands on some envelopes. Take a stack of envelopes and label each with a specific expense category. Fill these envelopes with the money you allocated for each expense, and you're all set! Whenever you need to spend money on a specific category, use only the cash from that envelope. For example, if you need to buy groceries, take money from the "groceries" envelope. Once the envelope is empty, you'll need to wait until the next budgeting period or until you can reallocate funds from another envelope.[46] It's simple but super-effective.

Reflection Questions

- What is the best strategy (for me) for tackling multiple debts?
- What are the different types of debt?

Putting It All Together

Understanding debt and the difference between good and bad debt is part of figuring out how money actually works. It's important to become financially literate; that way, you can effectively use various strategies and tips to handle debt and achieve financial stability. Knowing how to handle debt effectively is crucial if you want to save money. Saving the right way is not difficult, but it does take a bit of planning and discipline to pull off, but more on that in the next chapter.

CHAPTER 8

SAVING THE RIGHT WAY

Saving money as a young adult can be difficult due to limited income and numerous temptations to spend on things that don't add real value to your life. However, with planning and discipline, you can develop smart saving habits and grow your fortune. It's never too early to start saving, and once you understand the basics of personal finance, saving for your retirement as a teenager or college student is completely doable. That's what Zach Sprung did, after all!

Zach Sprung is a typical teen. He enjoys hockey, hangs out with friends, and does the things most teens do. What is not typical about

Zach is the deal he has with his father. For every dollar Zach saves for his retirement, his dad matches it with spending money. Talk about motivation! Having started this savings habit when he was 14; at 17, Zach is sitting back and "letting the compound interest do the work".[47] Zach did have a bit of help understanding the lingo of finance and the power of compound interest, as his father is a financial planner. Even if you don't have a family member who works in finance, it is still possible to give your financial future a boost by saving from an early age. Here's how to do it in a few easy steps:

Step One: Figure Out How Much You Need

Maybe you are saving for retirement like Zach did, or you are eyeing the latest smartphone or a snazzy pair of designer boots. Perhaps you are saving for your first car. Whatever you're saving for, you'll need to know how much you need first. Do some research to see where you can find the best deal. As soon as you have that magic number, aim to save more than that amount to cover any extras that may be needed (such as sales tax or protective casings).

Now it's time for a bit of math. Take the purchase amount of the item you want and subtract any savings you've already set aside.[48] Then divide the balance by the number of weeks until you can purchase. Let's say you want to buy a car in the next year for $10,000, and you already have $3,000 in your savings. You'll need to save a total of $7,000 to buy that sweet ride. Now, we take that $7,000 and divide it by 52 (the number of weeks in a year). This gives us $134.61. So, you'll need to put $134.61 away every week to reach the $10,000 goal. If it's not possible for you to save $134.61 every week, give yourself more time. Take that same $7,000 and divide it by 78 (the number of weeks in a year and a half), and you'll end up with a more manageable amount of $89.74 that you need to put away every week.

This easy bit of math works for any kind of purchase you want to make that you need to save for.

Step Two: Start Earning Money

You need to have three things in place if you want to save money: a bank account, a goal, and an income. Getting a part-time job as a babysitter, pet sitter, or burger flipper is one option, but there are other nontraditional options as well. One option is creating and selling items on Etsy.[49] You could even start a YouTube channel to earn income and sell merchandise. Whatever you choose to do, make sure that it is flexible enough to fit around your school schedule.

Step Three: Make a Budget

It's a good idea to separate your spending money from your savings, that way, you won't accidentally spend the cash you've been working so hard to save. In Chapter 5, the ins and outs of budgeting are discussed in detail, so I won't delve too deeply here. What is most important is that you draw up a budget and stick to it as best you can, so your savings will continue to grow. You'll need to calculate how much to set aside from your paycheck (as described in step one) to make the budget work. Don't hesitate to use apps to help you budget and save.

Step Four: Spending Trade-Offs

The trouble with money (whether it's cards or cash) is that it's difficult to keep track of how and where we spend it. To understand how you spend your money, consider keeping track of your spending for a month or two. You can use an app to help you, or you can do it the old-fashioned way by keeping a diary. Soon you'll be able to see where your money is going and how all those little purchases add up. Using the data from your diary or app, take a close look at your spending habits and decide where you can cut back.

Step Five: Find Ways to Make More Money

Not saving as much or as fast as you'd like? In that case, you might consider finding ways to make more money. If you have a part-time job, you could consider asking your supervisor for extra hours. You could even strike up a deal with your parents or guardians and take on a big project at home (such as cleaning out the garage, basement, or attic) in exchange for a bigger allowance. Or you could try your hand at a side gig, such as walking dogs, washing cars, or helping middle school kids with their homework.

Whatever you're saving for, it will be that much sweeter when you've reached it because you figured out a way to do it on your own. That's the first step to becoming truly independent and succeeding at "adulting."

TIPS FOR SAVING MONEY

Now that you've got a good idea of how to save toward a goal, it's time to share some tips that will help you maximize your savings.

- **"Pay yourself first" technique:** Whenever you receive money, set aside a portion of it for savings before doing anything else. You can make saving a priority by automatically transferring a fixed amount into a savings account. This habit will help you build a financial safety net and develop responsible money management skills.
- **Take advantage of student discounts:** Many places offer discounts to students, so make it a habit to carry your student ID and inquire about available discounts when shopping. You'll be surprised how much you can save!
- **Put cash gifts from birthdays and holidays directly into savings:** Instead of immediately spending cash gifts, deposit them directly into your savings account. Saving these unexpected windfalls will contribute to your long-term financial security.
- **Practice the 30-day rule to prevent impulse purchases:** Before making a nonessential purchase, wait 30 days. This rule gives you time to consider whether the purchase is truly necessary and aligns with your financial goals.

- **Minimize debt:** Avoid accumulating unnecessary debt, especially high-interest credit card debt. With student loans, make sure you're familiar with the conditions. Borrow only what you need and develop a plan to pay off the debt as soon as possible. Minimizing debt will help you maintain financial freedom and avoid long-term financial burdens.

BIG PURCHASES TO SAVE UP FOR IF YOU'RE UNDER 30

There are two big purchases most people under 30 make that they need to save up for: a college degree and a car. Many teens want to pursue a degree, but college does not come cheap. To be frank, a college education may not be the right choice for everyone. If you decide that college is the right choice for you, keep in mind that it is not necessarily your parents' responsibility to pay for it. Those words might be hard to hear, but the truth is it can be incredibly empowering to take ownership of your education and to pay for college out of your pocket. So, how do you go about making your higher education dreams a reality?

First up, you'll need to save for college. Start a savings habit when you're young, and you'll be able to navigate the financial challenges of higher education more comfortably. If you don't have any savings or want to maximize the cash you already have, consider the following as well:

- **Applying for scholarships:** If you excel in sports, academics, or extracurricular activities, consider applying for a scholarship.[50] Scholarships are basically free money that you don't have to pay back, but they do come with terms and conditions. Apply for any scholarship you are eligible for, even the small ones, and watch your college stack grow!
- **Take advantage of aid:** There is no shame in applying for aid. In fact, every aspiring college student should make it a point to fill out the Federal Student Aid (FAFSA) application. The application is free, and schools use this form to determine how much money they can offer each student. From work-study programs to school aid, FAFSA covers all kinds of things that can get you free money to study and is definitely worth a look. Know that FAFSA also indicates how big of a student loan you can get, so be sure to read the fine print when that award letter arrives.
- **Take advanced placement (AP) classes:** AP classes offer the chance to earn college credits while you're still in high school. This can translate into considerable savings, as every AP class taken is one less class you'll end up paying for in college. Your academic counselor can give you more information on this.
- **Learn the basics of paying for college:** Whether you have a full-time job or a side gig, it's important you master the basics of paying for college. Save your money whenever possible, and try to avoid student loans if possible. It may be your dream to attend Harvard or Princeton, but Ivy League schools can be extremely expensive. Plus, there are moving costs and travel expenses to think about too. Living at home and commuting to a local community college or state college can potentially save you thousands of dollars. Some companies also offer tuition reimbursement, so that's something to look into as well.

Considerations When Saving for a Car

Young and inexperienced drivers are far more likely to get into an accident, and there are statistics to back it up. In fact, teen drivers have a crash rate nearly four times higher than drivers older than 20.[51] It should come as no surprise then that insurance companies consider teen drivers high-risk, and with that comes higher premiums (monthly payments).

When you become a licensed driver, you'll need to get your own car insurance, or your parents can add you to their existing policy. Being added to an existing policy will increase the insurance premiums drastically, sometimes by 220%.[52] Insurance costs may drop as you grow older, gain experience, and maintain a clean driving record, but they still remain a big cost. Fortunately, there are things you can do to keep the insurance cost to an absolute minimum, including:

- Obeying traffic laws and driving safely.
- Shopping around for auto insurance to find the lowest prices.
- Reducing coverage limits or increasing deductibles in your policy (make sure you understand the trade-offs before you do this).
- Driving a car that's inexpensive to insure.
- Focusing on school and getting good grades; many companies offer discounts to good students.
- Taking defensive driving courses; insurance companies tend to reward drivers with discounts.

There's also the cost and maintenance of the vehicle to consider. Regular oil changes and tune-ups can become a pricey affair. Another consideration is the availability of spare parts. Eventually, something in your car will make a funny noise, or won't work like it should. That's understandable. Of all the hundreds of parts that make up a car, we can't expect everything to last an eternity. Cars can't be fixed with duct tape and a prayer; you'll need a skilled mechanic who is familiar with the type of vehicle you drive. However, the harder a spare part is to find, the more expensive it will be to replace, and mechanics don't work for free, either. The labor costs can add up drastically if your car is in the workshop for extended periods. So, before setting your heart on a specific car, do some digging to see if it's a practical ride for you at this stage in your life.

Exercise – Setting and Saving for a Financial Goal

1. **Identify Financial Goals:** List at least one financial goal you'd like to achieve in the short, medium, or long term. This goal should be specific, measurable, achievable, relevant, and time-bound (SMART). For example:
    - Short term (within 6 months): Saving for a new smartphone.
    - Medium term (1-2 years): Saving for a study abroad program.
    - Long term (3-5 years): Saving for a down payment on a car.
2. **Research Costs:** Once you've identified your goal, research the approximate costs associated with the goal. You can use online resources, ask for quotes, or use past experiences to estimate costs. Record these costs next to your goal.
3. **Assess Current Financial Situation:** You can do this by noting your income (allowance, part-time job, etc.) and any regular expenses (transportation, entertainment, etc.). This will

help you understand how much money you can realistically save each month.
4. **Determine Savings Timeline:** Based on your current financial situation and the cost of your goal, you can calculate how many months or years it'll take to save enough money for your goal. Be realistic with your projections.
5. **Create a Savings Plan:** This plan should outline:
   - How much you will save each month for your goal.
   - Where you will keep your savings (e.g., a separate bank account or a digital savings app).
   - Any adjustments you need to make in your spending habits to accommodate the savings plan.
6. **Monitor and Adjust:** Throughout your savings journey, regularly monitor your progress. Set up reminders to check your savings. If you encounter unexpected expenses or changes in your financial situation, adjust your savings plan accordingly.
7. **Reflect:** After a few weeks or months, reflect on your progress. Did you stick to your savings plan? Did you encounter any challenges? What did you learn from the experience? This reflection will help you understand your financial behaviors and make improvements for the future.
8. **Celebrate Milestones:** This could be reaching a certain percentage of your goal or achieving a mini-goal within the larger goal. Acknowledging your progress will help you stay motivated.

Reflection Questions

- What are the best ways to save money (for me)?
- How can I manage my money better and limit spending on unnecessary items?

PUTTING IT ALL TOGETHER

By using a step-by-step approach to saving money, setting financial goals, earning money through part-time jobs, creating a budget, making spending trade-offs, and increasing income, it is possible to save money as a young adult. Of course, it's much easier to reach those goals when you learn about the power of investing, so in the next chapter, we'll discuss how to do this.

CHAPTER 9

THE POWER OF INVESTING

Investing is a great way for young adults to build stability and wealth. But wealth doesn't just mean money; health is wealth, too.

INVESTING IN YOURSELF FIRST

When we invest in our *mental health*, our lives will become richer and fuller. The investment you make in your mental health today can be a gift that keeps on giving for many years to come. You're investing for a better tomorrow.

But wait... what exactly is mental health? It's simply the state of your psychological and emotional well-being. It's neither good nor bad, and it's not positive or negative. It doesn't necessarily mean mental illness either. Even though, I, Josh, live with mental illnesses (I have been diagnosed by a professional as having clinical depression and generalized anxiety disorder), these mental illnesses *can* affect my mental health but not always.

The first time I realized I needed to invest in my mental health was in 2011, just after turning 27 (though I wish I had learned about all this back in grade school). My dad passed away in 2009, at the time it felt like my family was falling apart, I had recently gone through a difficult breakup, I didn't know anything about mental health, I was going through a lot of major life changes, I was living with two undiagnosed mental illnesses (had I been getting treatment for them, I would have been fine), and to top it off, I started thinking nobody loved me or cared about me and the world would be better off if I weren't in it. Of course, now, I know that's not true, but my brain at that time was unwell. Thankfully, something inside me told me I needed to get help (the first time I intentionally took care of my mental health), and I did. I first reached out to family and friends and eventually a professional counselor. From there, I decided I needed to develop new tools to live life so I would:

a) Never get back to such a dark place,
b) Be able to deal with difficult things in a healthier way when they come up, and
c) Make peace of mind a habit and not just something to wish for.

Here are a just few ways you can invest in your mental health (which means investing in yourself):

- **Sleeping** - Getting on a semi-normal sleep cycle is huge (it definitely was for me). Instead of alternating falling asleep at midnight, the next night at 2 a.m., and the next at 6 a.m., try to get on the same schedule with few exceptions. Adults need seven to eight hours of sleep (young adults may need more), and missing out on regular sleep can have a negative effect on your emotions, your creativity, and the quality of your work. Taking all-nighters to cram is rarely useful. It's better to wake up feeling rested and then tackle your work.
- **Food** - I'm no nutritional expert, but I know that eating a whole extra-sausage extra-large pizza by yourself in one sitting is not great for your physical or mental health. What and how we eat can greatly influence our mental health. When we eat with the intention of food being a nourishing coping skill, we'll have a healthier body and healthier mind.
- **The Support of Positive People** - Studies have shown that *without* social support or with minimal social support, there is an increased risk of depression, alcohol use, suicide ideation and attempts, cardiovascular disease, and diminished brain function. I

used to hang with a mixed bag of people. But while learning to deal with depression in 2011, I realized I could only keep positive people around. Negative people drained my time and energy and put me in a bad place mentally. Positive people helped me see new possibilities and the good parts of myself and inspired me to raise my game as a friend, student, mentor, and entrepreneur.

- **Exercise and Movement** - When first learning about mental health, I noticed the extra endorphins produced during exercise helped change my brain chemistry for a short period. In some of my darkest moments, exercise provided temporary relief from the hurricane of negativity crashing about inside my brain. Light movement is totally fine—this isn't about losing weight or getting swole. Exercise helps improve memory and reduces symptoms of chronic stress.
- **Talking it Out** - Prior to 2011, I never talked to anyone about anything I was struggling with, and I rarely asked for help. But I had to change this to be able to go on living. And there are lots of ways to talk and get support. If your school has a counseling center, that could be a great place to start. You don't need a diagnosis to make an appointment. Identify people in your world who you feel safe with having a heart-to-heart.
- **Being Helpful and Giving Back** - Helping others provides a sense of meaning. In one sociological study, Americans who described themselves as "very happy" volunteered at least 5.8 hours per month. Another study showed that seniors who volunteered 200 hours per year decreased their risk for hypertension by 40 percent. You can help people in many different ways. Help a kid tie their shoe, provide meals to someone down on their luck, or work in public service. Do what you can, where you can, when you can.
- **Relaxation and Restoration** - Reading, journaling, drinking water, taking short but regular breaks (think: a walk around the house, 10 push-ups, stretching for 5 minutes, naps, or deep-

breathing), any form of meditation, reading, self-education, and mini-vacations are all forms of relaxing and restorative activities. Installing these practices in your life becomes easier when you create systems to set them up (as rituals).

FINANCIAL INVESTING 101

When it comes to financial wealth, much like mental health, the sooner you start investing, the better. The earlier you start investing your money, the more you can make from compound interest. Think of compound interest as a way to earn interest on both the money you originally put into an account and the interest you've already earned.[53] So, as time goes on, you not only earn interest on your initial money but also on the interest you've accumulated. It's a pretty cool mathematical principle that can increase your savings without requiring you to save more. Let me show you how this exciting principle works with an example.

Let's say you've got $100 in a savings account that gives you 5% interest per year. This translates to interest earnings of $5 in that first year. So, now you'll have $105 in the account, on which you'll earn 5% interest, which is $5.25. At the end of the second year, your account will have a balance of $110.25. That's $10.25 you've earned by literally doing nothing with your money in the account! As you keep going, your interest keeps growing because you keep earning interest on the interest you've already earned. This compounding effect makes your money grow faster and faster over time! It's a pretty cool "cheat code" to earn free money in the real world without lifting a finger.

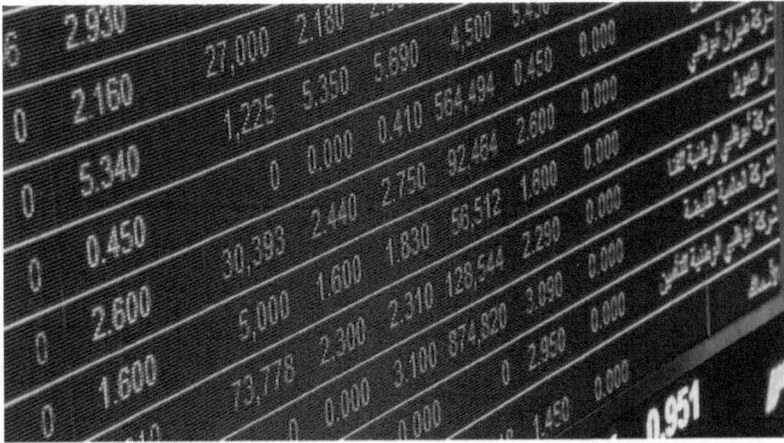

WHAT KIND OF INVESTOR WILL YOU BE?

Risky investments have the potential for big gains, but they can also lead to big losses. Low-risk investments are considered more of a safe bet, the risk of losing all your money is minimal, but the returns you'll get on them are minimal as well.[54] Both investment types can help you achieve your financial goals, but for the inexperienced investor, it is best to stick to low-risk investments.

When you've figured out what kind of investor you are (high-risk, a safe bet, or a mix of the two), you'll need to decide which investments are right for you. Different kinds of financial investments include (but are definitely not limited to):

- **Stocks:** One of the reasons companies sell stock is to raise funds. Stocks are small bits of ownership in a company.[55] As the company grows and makes profits, its stock value increases, meaning you can sell your stocks for a higher price. But there are two sides to every coin, so if the company does poorly, its stock prices will go down, which can result in a loss. Investing in individual stocks can be risky, so it is vital to do your research and choose wisely.
- **Bonds:** When you buy a bond, you're basically lending your money to the issuer for a set period. In return, the issuer pays you interest on that money.[56] Once the bond reaches its maturity date,

the issuer gives you back the original amount you lent. Bonds are generally considered safer than stocks because they offer a more predictable return.

- **Funds:** This is a way to invest in a bunch of different stocks (or bonds) at the same time. A professional fund manager makes the investment for you. There are two common types of funds: mutual funds and exchange-traded funds (ETFs). Mutual funds are bought and sold through the fund company, while ETFs are traded on the stock exchange like individual stocks.[57] Funds are a popular choice because they help diversify your investment portfolio.
- **High-yield savings accounts:** Think of them as super-charged savings accounts. They're like a regular savings account but with a higher interest rate. It's a super safe place to keep your money, but the returns are lower when compared to stocks and bonds.
- **Certificates of Deposit (CD):** Certificates of deposit are like savings accounts with a twist. You agree to leave your money in the bank for a fixed period of time. In return, the bank gives you a higher interest rate than a regular savings account.[58] It's an incredibly safe option because your money is insured, however, the catch is that you can't touch your cash until the CD matures. Penalties may apply if you do. CDs are good for money you don't need to use right away and want to grow safely.

Exercise – Dipping Your Toes in the Water of Investing

After you've learned a bit about investing and figured out what type of investor you are, you'll need to do some research to find the right investment opportunities for you. Research and explore companies that align with your interests and investment goals. Dig into their financials and growth potential to build a list of companies you'd like to own. You can also look at top money market accounts or CDs currently offering the best rates. Once you have researched the basics, you are three small steps away from making your very first investment.

Test the Waters with a Mock Portfolio/Simulated Investing

Before committing your money to the void, try investing in a safe and risk-free way. Make use of a practice account to make virtual investments. This way, you can see how your investments would perform without any actual financial risk. It's like playing a game where you pretend to invest and see how your money grows or declines in value over time. This allows you to learn about investing without risk.

Open and Fund a Real Brokerage Account

Once you're ready to invest, open a brokerage account. If you're under 18, seek assistance from a parent or guardian to open a custodial account.[59] The process is quite simple, and a Roth IRA for kids can be a great start if you have earned income.

Make Your First Investment

When your funds are ready, make your first investment purchase. Choose from the companies on your list or a bond or a CD, and set up a market order. Keep adding to your investments to build a diversified portfolio over time, harnessing the power of compound interest for your financial future.

REFLECTION QUESTIONS

- What forms of investments do young people typically handle?
- How can I find more information about how to invest as a young adult?

PUTTING IT ALL TOGETHER

There are many investment opportunities for young adults out there. The best part of all is that if you start a savings and investing habit early, you can have compound interest do the heavy lifting for you for far longer than adults who step late into the investing game. Of course, whenever we earn income, taxes become an important consideration. In the next chapter, we'll take a look at what you need to do to stay in the taxman's good books.

CHAPTER 10

WHAT ABOUT TAXES?

As a young adult, filing taxes can seem intimidating, but if you understand the basics and are organized about gathering your paperwork and submitting your forms, you can get through the process easily and with few headaches.

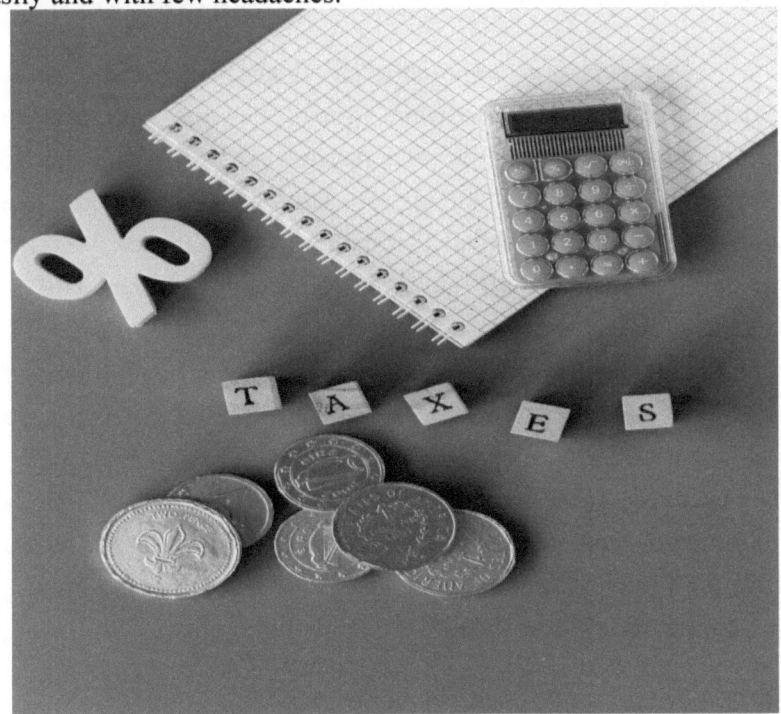

Taxes can be confusing for anyone! However, there are a few things you need to know that can make submitting tax returns a lot easier. Generally, the IRS (Internal Revenue Service) expects people under the age of 65 to file if they earn more than the standard deduction amount for that year. Even when you earn less than the standard deduction amount, you might be owed a refund if your employer withholds money from your paycheck for tax purposes. So, it's always a good idea to get your tax affairs in order.

When filing taxes, it's vital that your parents or guardians do not report your income on their tax returns. However, the IRS mandates that you state on your return that another person may list you as a dependent.[60] If you earn more than $400 per year, you may need to file a tax return, as the IRS considers you self-employed.

The Difference Between Net Income and Gross Income

Every working person is supposed to pay federal taxes and contribute to Social Security and Medicare (Social Security and Medicare contributions will show up on your paystub as "FICA"). Some state governments charge an income tax too. These taxes come directly out of your paycheck and are called "withholding".[61] As a result, your take-home pay (net income) will never be equal to the amount you earn (gross income).

The tax rate determines how much tax you owe. In addition to the tax rate, it's good to know which tax bracket you fall into. But taxes are not all about taking money from your paycheck! Sometimes you get money back too. These are called tax refunds or rebates. The IRS uses the information you submit in your tax return to determine if you are eligible for a refund. Typically, if an employer withholds too much tax from your paycheck, you should be eligible for a rebate.

What Young Adults Should Know About Doing Taxes

Before you jump into the deep end of trying to figure this tax thing out, it's important to know a few basics. Tax Day usually falls on April 15th. If the 15th is a weekend or public holiday, the IRS will announce a new date. The taxes due on this day are for the previous calendar year ending on December 31st.[62] Next, you need to ask yourself a few important questions:

- How much money did you make last year?
- What is your marital status? (Mark "single" on the tax form if you are not married.)
- Did your parents or guardians list you as a dependent?
- Does your state collect income tax?
- Did your employer withhold taxes from your paycheck?

Now you'll need a W-2 form and other important tax documents. These usually become available online in January. It's always a good idea to start early on your tax return. Often, you won't know beforehand if you are eligible for a refund or need to pay additional taxes. So, you should ensure you've got a small pile of cash to pay any outstanding taxes you may owe. Other important things to keep in mind as you are working through your tax form include:

- **Knowing your tax classification:** Tax reporting is different for employees and freelancers (or independent contractors). Employees will need to complete a W-4 form when they start the job and will receive a W-2 later in the year. If you're a freelancer, gig worker, or entrepreneur, you'll be responsible for reporting and paying self-employment taxes. In this case, you'll need to fill out a W-9 form to receive a 1099 later in the year.
- **Check if your parents/guardians claim you as a dependent:** If you're still in college, your parents or guardians may claim you as a dependent in return for tax

benefits. If you are listed as a dependent, you'll need to indicate this on your tax form.
- **State taxes:** Some states require you to file a state tax return in addition to your regular tax return. The details will vary by state, so you'll need to find out what your state's stance on taxes is.
- **Student loans:** You could deduct a tidy sum from your taxes if your modified adjusted gross income (MAGI) is under a certain threshold.[63] However, if you are using an employee assistance program to study, you might not qualify for a deduction. Make sure to include the 1098-E form in your tax returns.
- **Scholarships and grants:** These are considered tax-free and are not part of your income. If you used any part of the scholarship to pay for your room or other student expenses, you'll need to include these amounts as part of your taxable income.

You've got a few options when it comes to filing your tax return. If your return is straightforward, you can generally file your taxes for free.[64] You can also get help from the IRS Volunteer Income Tax Assistance Program or work with a tax preparation service to ensure your tax game is on point.

Special Tax Rules for Minors

Let's talk about special tax rules for a minute. If you have income from things like dividends or interest (which the IRS calls "unearned income"), there's a limit. For example, if you made more than $1,150 in 2022, you'll need to file a tax return. But if you have both earned and unearned income, you'll need to add them up to see if you need to file. Then there's *Kiddie Tax*. This is a special tax rule that applies to the unearned income of certain young people, typically children who are under the age of 18 or full-time students under the age of 24.[65] This rule was designed to prevent parents from taking advantage of lower tax rates by shifting investment income to their children.

Even if you earn less than the limits, there are a couple of other situations where you might still need to file. For instance, if you owe Social Security or Medicare taxes on tip income or if you have income from self-employment and make $400 or more in 2022.

Here's something cool: If you need to file a tax return for unearned income, your parents can choose to claim it on their own return instead. But there are some rules to follow, like a limit on the amount of money involved. Just use Form 8814 with your parents'/guardians' 1040 tax form, and the IRS won't make you file separately.[66]

Exercise (Review) – Callie's Summer Job, Prepping for Taxes

Callie is a 19-year-old college student who just finished her summer job as a lifeguard at a local pool. She earned $5,000 over the summer. She wants to learn about taxes and how to file her tax return. Let's guide her through the process of filling out a simplified tax return.

Step 1: Gather Information

Before Callie starts filling out her tax return, she needs to gather some important information:

1. **W-2 Form:** Callie's employer provided her with a W-2 form, which shows her total earnings and the amount of taxes withheld during the year.
2. **Social Security Number (SSN):** This is a unique identifier used for tax purposes.

Step 2: Determine Filing Status

Callie is a single college student, so her filing status is "Single."

Step 3: Calculate Gross Income

Callie's gross income is the total amount she earned before any deductions. In this case, it's the $5,000 she earned from her summer job.

Step 4: Calculate Adjusted Gross Income (AGI)

AGI is the amount of income left after subtracting specific deductions, known as "above-the-line" deductions. Since Callie doesn't have any above-the-line deductions in this scenario, her AGI is the same as her gross income, which is $5,000.

Step 5: Calculate Taxable Income

Taxable income is the amount used to calculate how much tax Callie owes. It's calculated by subtracting standard deduction (or itemized deductions) from her AGI.

Since this is a simplified scenario, and we'll use the standard deduction for a single filer, let's assume the standard deduction is $6,000.

Taxable Income = AGI - Standard Deduction Taxable Income = $5,000 - $6,000 = $0 (Callie's taxable income is $0)

Step 6: Calculate Tax Owed

In this scenario, Callie's taxable income is $0, which means she doesn't owe any federal income tax.

Step 7: Calculate Refund or Tax Due

Since Callie's tax owed is $0 and she had taxes withheld from her paycheck, she is eligible for a tax refund.

Step 8: Complete the Tax Return Form

Callie will need to complete a simplified tax return form, such as the 1040-EZ. On the form, she'll provide her personal information, filing status, income details, and calculate her refund.

Step 9: Submit the Tax Return

Callie can file her tax return electronically or by mail. Since she's expecting a refund, filing electronically will likely result in a faster refund.

Reflection Questions

- How do teens or college students file taxes?
- Are there any special deductions or credits available to college students or teens?

Putting It All Together

Taxes can be scary if you don't know what you are supposed to do. Knowing your filing status and how to fill out a tax form are the basics for being an independent adult and becoming financially literate. Don't hesitate to get help if you are uncertain about what to do with your taxes. It's better to play it safe and submit a return (and possibly get a rebate) than end up in the taxman's bad books. Filing your taxes on time is a big responsibility, but just as important is preparing yourself for rainy days.

CHAPTER 11

PLANNING FOR RAINY DAYS

As a young adult, you may need different types of insurance depending on your lifestyle and financial situation. Insurance can be puzzling, but in this chapter, I'll try to solve that mystery once and for all.

Let's start with what insurance is. It's there to catch you and your loved ones if something bad goes down, like a fire, theft, getting sued, or getting into a car wreck. When you get insurance, you get a legal agreement called an insurance policy with the company. If something happens that's covered by your policy, you can file a claim, and they'll pay you or your beneficiaries based on the terms of the policy.[67] It's a pretty sweet deal, right?

The tricky part about insurance is that you are paying for something you hope you'll never need. Nobody wants bad things to happen, but when something does go wrong, such as getting into a car crash, it can leave you in an incredibly tough spot financially. So, insurance is there to cover your six when you need it most.

Now, let's talk about the advantages of having insurance. It's a pretty cool financial tool and can give you peace of mind knowing you'll get help should some unforeseen event take place. It may assist you in getting back on track faster.

Your insurance agent can be super helpful, too. They can explain all the perks of your insurance and let you know about any extra benefits you might have. Some policies might give you free roadside assistance, help with business risks, or even some cash value with life insurance. Plus, in some cases, it's the law to have insurance. If you are driving, you'll need insurance for your car. In the workplace, workers' compensation can help protect others.

How Insurance Works

Now that you've got a clearer picture of what insurance is, it's time to discuss how it actually works. Think of it as a huge rainy-day fund that's shared by lots of people (policyholders) and managed by the insurance company. The company collects money from its policyholders (that's the premium you pay), and they use it to run their business and cover the costs when people make claims. Since disasters are unpredictable, like tornadoes, hailstorms, wildfires, or just regular fender benders and kitchen fires, the insurance company's main goal is to stay financially strong so they can handle whatever comes their way.

When choosing an insurance provider, consider the following:
- Check out their insurance coverage. Do they offer the types of insurance you need, and can you get a discount if you bundle them all together?

- Look at their financial strength. You want to make sure they can actually pay up if you need to make a claim. Check out U.S. credit rating agency AM Best for this information.
- Decide if you want a local insurance agent's help or if you're good with managing things on your own.
- Listen to what other people are saying about the company in online reviews and see if they recommend it.

When you're unsure about something, just hit up your local independent insurance agent. They're the experts and can guide you through the whole insurance process and help you find the best coverage for you, your family, and everything you care about.

Exercise (Review) - Insurance Checklist for Young Adults

Every young adult will need insurance, for sure. With so many insurance options out there, it can be hard to decide what to get. To make things easier, here are five essential insurance types you'll need soon or in the near future:

1. **Renters insurance:** This insurance covers your belongings in case of theft, fire, or even water damage. Imagine your laptop, TV, and all the cool gadgets you own getting destroyed—talk about a nightmare! Renters insurance swoops in to save the day and helps you replace your things.
2. **Auto insurance:** Before you tear up the tarmac with your car, you need to make sure you have auto insurance. This is like a safety net for your car. If you accidentally crash into something or someone scratches your ride, auto insurance will come to the rescue and cover the repairs. Not to mention, if you cause an accident and others get hurt, this insurance will help cover their medical bills and the legal stuff.
3. **Personal liability insurance:** Let's say you accidentally break someone's expensive gadget or someone gets injured on your property. Personal liability insurance steps up to pay for the

damages and medical expenses, saving you from a financial disaster.[68] It's like having a safety cushion for those unexpected curveballs life throws at us sometimes.

4. **Health insurance:** College can be fun, but it can be a wild ride too. You never know when you might catch the "freshman flu" or slip on a wet surface. Health insurance comes in handy when your body takes a beating, helping to cover your medical bills, doctor visits, prescription drugs, and even those hospital stays that can quickly drain your savings.

5. **Life insurance:** This is a safety net for your loved ones, especially in the event something happens to you. If the worst were to happen, life insurance would help your family financially by giving them a lump sum of money. They can use it to cover expenses like funeral costs, debts, or even future college fees for your siblings.[69]

Reflection Questions

- What is insurance?
- What kind of insurance do I need as a young adult?

Putting it All Together

Life happens. There's no stopping the unpredictable moments in life, but with the right insurance, you can navigate those uncertain times with a measure of financial ease. Of course, when it comes to building long-term wealth, there are a few principles you need to adhere to, but more on that in the next chapter.

CHAPTER 12

BUILDING A FUTURE OF WEALTH

Long-term financial responsibility is a vital component of the overall wealth-building strategy. It means not only developing a plan for saving and investing money over time but also making sure you stick to that plan to give you the best chance of achieving financial success. It takes discipline, patience, and a whole lot of hustle. So, stay focused, keep learning, and make those money moves wisely. It also helps to stick to the principles of long-term financial responsibility. These principles have been covered in depth in the previous chapters, but here's a quick recap:

- **Make strategic investment decisions:** Building long-term wealth isn't just about saving up every penny you earn. You've got to be a smart cookie when it comes to investing your hard-earned cash. Do your research, stay informed about market trends, and diversify your portfolio to gain maximum benefit from investing. Don't put all your eggs in one basket. Spread them out across different investment options like stocks, bonds, real estate, or mutual funds. Investment is a long-term game, not a get-rich-quick scheme.

- **Use credit cards wisely:** Credit cards can be your best friend or your worst enemy, depending on how you use them. You have to be disciplined and refrain from going on wild spending sprees. Treat your credit card like a lifeline, not a license to splurge. Pay your bills on time and in full so you don't end up drowning in debt. High interest rates can eat you alive! Use credit cards responsibly, and they'll reward you with perks and build your credit score, which is like your financial street cred. You don't want it to be in tatters.

- **Live within your means:** This means spending less than you earn. Don't try to keep up with the Kardashians or live a champagne lifestyle on a beer budget. Be honest with yourself about what you can afford, and set a budget that keeps you on track.[70] Yes, it might mean skipping that fancy restaurant or waiting a bit longer to upgrade your phone, but it's all about delayed gratification. Save for the future and avoid unnecessary debt like the plague.

- **Consider starting your own business:** If you've got that entrepreneurial itch, don't be afraid to scratch it. Starting your own business can be a real game-changer for your financial future. It's a wild ride, no doubt, but it comes with the potential for big rewards. Identify your passion, find a problem to solve, or spot an untapped market, and then dive in headfirst. Sure, there'll be ups and downs, but the satisfaction of building something from scratch and the freedom to be your own boss are worth it. Plus, if it takes off, it can be a major source of wealth down the road.

- **Always have an emergency fund:** Life is full of surprises, and not all of them are good ones. Unexpected car repairs, medical emergencies, or even a sudden job loss—life can throw you some curveballs—but with an emergency fund, you'll be ready to take them on without going gray from all the stress. Aim to save up at least three to six months' worth of living expenses in a separate account.[71] This way, you won't have to rely on credit cards or loans when life throws you a curveball. Peace of mind is priceless!

- **Be proactive about your mental health:** Taking care of your mental health isn't just about feeling better in the moment; it's an investment in your future. When you prioritize your mental well-being, you're setting the stage for a richer life, both emotionally and financially. A healthy mind helps you stay focused, make better decisions, and build stronger relationships. It allows you to pursue your goals with resilience and creativity, paving the way for success and financial stability. Being proactive about your mental health is an essential step on the path to becoming wealthy, not just in your bank account but in life's true riches.

PUTTING IT ALL TOGETHER

Building long-term wealth is a journey that requires discipline, patience, and some good old-fashioned hustle. By sticking to the principles we've covered, you'll be well on your way to achieving financial success. Well done for making it this far! By making it through this book, you've taken a significant step toward securing your financial future and building long-term wealth. As you embark on your journey to build your fortune, remember these lessons. It's not always easy, but staying focused and continuing to learn will set you on the path to financial success.

The ball is in your court now. Take a moment to envision what you want your future to look like, and identify the most important goals for yourself. Be specific and create a plan to achieve them step by step.

Before we part ways, feel free to leave a review and feedback on Amazon. Your thoughts will help others discover this book and embark on their financial journey with confidence. And if I can help in any other way or if you just want to say "hi," you can get in touch with me on LinkedIn or social media (I'm pretty easy to find) or via www.iampossibleproject.com.

I want to wish you the best of luck on your journey to financial freedom. It won't always be easy, but stay determined, stay disciplined, and remember that you have the power to shape your financial destiny. With the knowledge you've gained from this book, you can achieve anything you set your mind to.

REFERENCES

1 - Jacimovic, D. (2022, September 7). *25+ educational financial literacy statistics you need to learn about.* Moneytransfers. https://moneytransfers.com/news/2022/09/07/financial-literacy-statistics

2 - Thielen, P. (2023, March 14). *Council post: the connection between financial well-being and mental health.* Forbes. https://www.forbes.com/sites/forbesfinancecouncil/2023/03/14/the-connection-between-financial-well-being-and-mental-health/#:~:text=Mental%20health%20and%20financial%20well

3 - World Health Organization. (n.d.). *Reduced number of people suffering financial hardship.* https://www.who.int/about/accountability/results/who-results-report-2020-2021/outcome/2021/reduced-number-of-people-suffering-financial-hardship-results-report-achievements

4 - *Personal finance.* (n.d.). Stride. https://peritumagri.com/stride/mod/page/view.php?id=15225

5, 8 - Murphy, W. (2021, August 3). *Why is personal finance important?* Clever Girl Finance. https://www.clevergirlfinance.com/why-is-personal-finance-important/

6 - *Stress in America 2020.* (2020). American Psychological Association. https://www.apa.org/news/press/releases/stress/2020/sia-mental-health-crisis.pdf

7 - Schlachtmeyer, L. (2015). *The teenage years are for practicing money decisions in a safe space.* Consumer Financial Protection Bureau. https://www.consumerfinance.gov/about-us/blog/the-teenage-years-are-for-practicing-money-decisions-in-a-safe-space/

9 - Ryu, S., & Fan, L. (2022). The relationship between financial worries and psychological distress among U.S. adults. *Journal of Family and Economic Issues, 44*(1), 16–33. https://doi.org/10.1007/s10834-022-09820-9

10 - Board of Governors of the Federal Reserve System. (2023). *Economic well-being of U.S. households in 2022.* Federal Reserve. https://www.federalreserve.gov/publications/files/2022-report-economic-well-being-us-households-202305.pdf

11 - Weber, M. (2023, June 6). *Coping with financial stress.* Helpguide.org. https://www.helpguide.org/articles/stress/coping-with-financial-stress.htm#:~:text=A%20number%20of%20studies%20have

12 - St Peter, E. (2019, January 17). *Financial stress linked to heart disease risk among African-Americans.* Harvard Gazette. https://news.harvard.edu/gazette/story/2019/01/financial-stress-linked-to-heart-disease-risk-among-african-americans/

13 - Smith, L. (2023, April 25). *How to learn about finance.* Investopedia. https://www.investopedia.com/articles/basics/11/become-self-taught-finance-expert.asp

14, 16 - Vitug, J. (2021, January 5). *Are you unconsciously spending on likes not loves?* Phroogal Financial Wellness. https://www.phroogal.com/money-mindset-unconsciously-spending-likes-not-loves/

15 - Gillespie, C. (2022, February 8). *Emotional spending was a common pandemic coping mechanism, experts say.* Verywell Mind. https://www.verywellmind.com/emotional-spending-5217055

17 - Pant, P. (2022, June 20). *Wants vs. needs: understanding the difference.* The Balance. https://www.thebalancemoney.com/how-to-separate-wants-and-needs-453592

18 - Cherry, K. (2021, April 29). *Why cultivating a growth mindset can boost your success*. Verywell Mind. https://www.verywellmind.com/what-is-a-mindset-2795025

19, 21 - Miranda, D. (n.d.). *You don't have to change your money mindset if you don't want to*. Healthyrich. https://www.healthyrich.co/p/money-mindset

20 - *Developing a money mindset*. (2023, July 6). My Millennial Money. https://www.mymillennial.money/blog/developing-a-money-mindset

22 - Fulciniti, F. (2020, January 4). *Should you really get a job as a teen? why and why not?* Prepscholar. https://blog.prepscholar.com/should-you-really-get-a-job-as-a-teen

23 - Doyle, A. (2021, August 19). *How to get your first part-time job for teens*. The Balance. https://www.thebalancemoney.com/tips-for-getting-your-first-part-time-job-2058650

24 - Sharkey, S. (2023, March 6). *How to make money as a teenager: 36 lucrative ways*. Clever Girl Finance. https://www.clevergirlfinance.com/how-to-make-money-as-a-teenager/

25 - Schwahn, L., & Tindall, T. (2023, March 28). *12 ways to make money as a kid*. NerdWallet. https://www.nerdwallet.com/article/finance/make-money-as-a-kid

26 - *How to make money as a teen—20 ideas to get started*. (2022, July 29). Greenlight. https://greenlight.com/blog/how-to-make-money-as-a-teen-20-ideas-to-get-started

27 - Fontinelle, A. (2022, February 24). *Banking 101*. Investopedia. https://www.investopedia.com/personal-finance/banking-101/

28 - *The Fed—how long is the lifespan of U.S. paper money?* (2013). Board of Governors of the Federal Reserve System. https://www.federalreserve.gov/faqs/how-long-is-the-life-span-of-us-paper-money.htm

29 - Flitter, E., & Agrawal, T. (2013, May 11). *Prepaid debit cards: a weak link in bank security*. Reuters. https://www.reuters.com/article/us-usa-crime-cybercrime-prepaidcards-idUKBRE94912G20130511

30 - FDIC. (2019). *FDIC: Federal deposit insurance corporation*. FDIC. https://www.fdic.gov/

31 - *4 most common types of bank accounts*. (2022, December 9). Ramsey Solutions. https://www.ramseysolutions.com/banking/types-of-bank-accounts

32 - Lake, R. (2019, August 21). *Debit cards vs. credit cards for teens*. US News. https://money.usnews.com/credit-cards/articles/debit-cards-vs-credit-cards-for-teens

33 - Altus, A. (2022, September 13). *Study: more than one in four Americans say their debt is unmanageable*. OppLoans. https://www.opploans.com/oppu/articles/personal-finance-study-2022/

34 - Mydoh. (2023, May 3). *Budgeting for teens: how to budget and tips for parents*. Mydoh. https://www.mydoh.ca/learn/money-101/money-basics/budgeting-101-a-guide-for-parents-and-teenagers/

35 - *How to create a zero-based budget*. (2023, May 31). Ramsey Solutions. https://www.ramseysolutions.com/budgeting/how-to-make-a-zero-based-budget

36 - *How to teach teenagers about money*. (2022, December 22). Ramsey Solutions. https://www.ramseysolutions.com/relationships/teach-teenagers-about-money

37 - Maiti, R. (2022, December 1). *Fast fashion: its detrimental effect on the environment*. Earth.org. https://earth.org/fast-fashions-detrimental-effect-on-the-environment/#:~:text=The%20Dark%20Side%20of%20Fast

38, 40 - Kiehl, E. (2023, May 23). *How do credit scores work?* Step. https://step.com/money-101/post/how-do-credit-scores-work-a-guide-for-teens

39 - Taylor, D. (2022, October 28). *The hidden history of your credit scores (and why it matters)*. WalletGenius. https://walletgenius.com/credit/the-hidden-history-of-your-credit-scores-and-why-it-matters/

41 - *How teenagers and young adults can establish a healthy credit score*. (2022). One Main Financial. https://www.onemainfinancial.com/resources/credit/how-teenagers-and-young-adults-can-establish-a-healthy-credit-score

42 - *How does a college degree improve graduates' employment and earnings potential?* (n.d.). The Association of Public and Land-Grant Universities. https://www.aplu.org/our-work/4-policy-and-advocacy/publicuvalues/employment-earnings/#66

43 - *What teens should know about good debt & bad debt.* (2022, July 12). Getschooled.com. https://getschooled.com/article/5785-good-debt-vs-bad-debt/

44, 45 - Mydoh. (2022, September 19). *How to pay off debt fast: a guide for parents and teens.* Mydoh. https://www.mydoh.ca/learn/money-101/debt/how-to-pay-off-debt-fast-a-guide-for-parents-and-teens/

46 - Cruze, R. (2023, June 23). *How to budget with the cash envelope system.* Ramsey Solutions. https://www.ramseysolutions.com/budgeting/envelope-system-explained

47 - Mitra, M. (2020, November 23). *Meet the teens saving for retirement.* Money. https://money.com/teenagers-retirement-savings-roth-ira/

48 - Bank of America. (n.d.). *Teen guide: 5 steps to saving for something you really want.* Better Money Habits. https://bettermoneyhabits.bankofamerica.com/en/saving-budgeting/saving-money-as-a-teenager

49 - Knueven, L. (2022, December 9). *How to save money as a teenager in 9 steps, so you can get yourself a car, pay for college, or take a trip.* Business Insider. https://www.businessinsider.com/personal-finance/how-to-save-money-as-a-teenager

50 - Ellis, K. (2023, February 17). *10 best ways to save for college.* Ramsey Solutions. https://www.ramseysolutions.com/saving/saving-for-college-is-easier-than-you-think

51 - Insurance Institute for Highway Safety (IIHS). (2017). *Teenagers.* IIHS-HLDI Crash Testing and Highway Safety. https://www.iihs.org/topics/teenagers

52 - Cook, V., & Blacklock, A. (2022, June 30). *15 best ways to save on car insurance for teens.* Women Who Money. https://womenwhomoney.com/save-money-teen-car-insurance/

53 - *How does compound interest work?* (n.d.). Securian Financial. https://www.securian.com/insights-tools/articles/how-compound-interest-works.html

54 - Hayes, M. (2022, March 2). *Low-risk vs high-risk investments*. Experian. https://www.experian.com/blogs/ask-experian/low-vs-high-risk-investments/#:~:text=Riskier%20investments%20have%20the%20potential

55 - Caldera, L. (2022, October 5). *The stock market explained for kids*. Kids' Money. https://www.kidsmoney.org/kids/investing/stock-market/

56 - Fernando, J. (2023a, March 9). *Bond: financial meaning with examples and how they are priced*. Investopedia. https://www.investopedia.com/terms/b/bond.asp

57 - Voigt, K., & Benson, A. (2023, March 29). *Mutual funds: what they are and how to invest*. NerdWallet. https://www.nerdwallet.com/article/investing/how-to-invest-in-mutual-funds

58 - Fernando, J. (2023b, May 3). *What is a certificate of deposit (CD) and what can it do for you?* Investopedia. https://www.investopedia.com/terms/c/certificateofdeposit.asp

59 - Whiteman, L. (2023, March 31). *Investment guide for teens and parents with teens*. The Motley Fool. https://www.fool.com/investing/how-to-invest/investing-for-teens/

60 - Taxslayer Editorial Team. (2023, February 7). *Taxes for teens—a beginner's guide*. TaxSlayer. https://www.taxslayer.com/blog/teen-filing-first-tax-return/

61 - Kagan, J. (2023, March 31). *Withholding tax explained: types and how it's calculated*. Investopedia. https://www.investopedia.com/terms/w/withholdingtax.asp

62 - Fishman, M. (2022, September 20). *What college students need to know about doing their taxes*. CNBC. https://www.cnbc.com/2022/08/17/what-college-students-need-to-know-about-doing-their-taxes.html

63 - Welding, L. (2023, June 9). *Tax filing guide: filing taxes as a student.* Best Colleges. https://www.bestcolleges.com/resources/college-student-tax-filing-guide/

64 - Lankford, K. (2023, February 28). *Tax filing tips for college students.* US News. https://money.usnews.com/money/personal-finance/taxes/articles/tax-filing-tips-for-college-students

65 - Kagan, J. (2021, December 5). *Kiddie tax definition.* Investopedia. https://www.investopedia.com/terms/k/kiddietax.asp

66 - *At what income does a minor have to file an income tax return?* (2022, May 11). Turbotax. https://turbotax.intuit.com/tax-tips/family/at-what-income-does-a-minor-have-to-file-an-income-tax-return/L6HOdGp6i

67 - *What is insurance and why is it important?* (n.d.). Grange Insurance. https://www.grangeinsurance.com/tips/what-is-insurance-why-is-it-important

68 - Dendas, B. (2018, December 12). *4 types of insurance every college student needs.* Pawson Insurance. https://pawson.com/4-types-of-insurance-every-college-student-needs/

69 - *The five types of insurance every college student needs.* (2021, July 16). Insurance Neighbor. https://www.insuranceneighbor.com/five-types-insurance-every-college-student-needs/

70 - Smith, L. (2019). *The basics of financial responsibility.* Investopedia. https://www.investopedia.com/articles/pf/09/financial-responsibility.asp

71 - Azam, S. (2023, April 26). *How to build an emergency fund on a low salary: tips and techniques.* Hubble. https://www.myhubble.money/blog/how-to-build-an-emergency-fund-on-a-low-salary-tips-and-techniques

IMAGE REFERENCES

Chapter 1

Pixabay. (2016d). *Coins on brown wood.* Pexels. https://www.pexels.com/photo/antique-bills-business-cash-210600/

Grabowska, K. (2020). *Close-up photo of banknotes under a calculator*. Pexels. https://www.pexels.com/photo/close-up-photo-of-banknotes-under-a-calculator-5942528/

Chapter 2

Ovan. (2016). *Black and white laptop computer.* Pexels. https://www.pexels.com/photo/black-and-white-laptop-computer-62689/

Miroshnichenko, T. (2021b). *Woman in blue plaid long sleeves and knit cap holding a glass jar with money.* Pexels. https://www.pexels.com/photo/woman-in-blue-plaid-long-sleeves-and-knit-cap-holding-a-glass-jar-with-money-7009596/

Chapter 3

Cottonbro Studio. (2020). *Person holding black tablet computer.* Pexels. https://www.pexels.com/photo/person-holding-black-tablet-computer-5989943/

Chapter 4

Expect Best. (2017). *Buildings with glass windows.* Pexels. https://www.pexels.com/photo/buildings-with-glass-windows-351264/

Shvets, A. (2020). *Person holding bank card.* Pexels. https://www.pexels.com/photo/person-holding-bank-card-4482900/

Pixabay. (2016c). *Blue master card on denim pocket.* Pexels. https://www.pexels.com/photo/blue-master-card-on-denim-pocket-164571/

Chapter 5

Miroshnichenko, T. (2021a). *Banknotes and calculator on table.* Pexels. https://www.pexels.com/photo/banknotes-and-calculator-on-table-6694543/

Pixabay. (2016b). *Black calculator near ballpoint pen on white printed paper.* Pexels. https://www.pexels.com/photo/black-calculator-near-ballpoint-pen-on-white-printed-paper-53621/

Chapter 6

PhotoMIX Company. (2016). *Documents on wooden surface.* Pexels. https://www.pexels.com/photo/documents-on-wooden-surface-95916/

Chapter 7

Nilov, M. (2021). *A man looking at the paper while holding a coffee and phone.* Pexels. https://www.pexels.com/photo/a-man-looking-at-the-paper-while-holding-a-coffee-and-phone-6963043/

Barts, N. (2021). *Man sitting on sofa and reading unpaid bills.* Pexels. https://www.pexels.com/photo/man-sitting-on-sofa-and-reading-unpaid-bills-7926655/

Chapter 8

Dovis. (2021). *Shattered pink piggy bank.* Pexels. https://www.pexels.com/photo/shattered-pink-piggy-bank-6719878/

Volquardsen, M. (2019). *White Harvard campus services truck.* Pexels. https://www.pexels.com/photo/white-harvard-campus-services-truck-2350924/

von Hoerst, S. (2019). *Photo of Montero Sport parked on grass field.* Pexels. https://www.pexels.com/photo/photo-of-montero-sport-parked-on-grass-field-2676096/

Chapter 9

Pixabay. (2017). *Numbers on monitor.* Pexels. https://www.pexels.com/photo/airport-bank-board-business-534216/

Chapter 10

Vaitkevich, N. (2021). *Notebook and calculator on green surface.* Pexels. https://www.pexels.com/photo/notebook-and-calculator-on-green-surface-6863180/

Chapter 11

Kindel Media. (2021). *A paper beside a person typing on a laptop.* Pexels. https://www.pexels.com/photo/a-paper-beside-a-person-typing-on-a-laptop-7688374/

Chapter 12

Pixabay. (2016a). *Banknotes and coins beside gray safety box.* Pexels. https://www.pexels.com/photo/bank-banknotes-bills-business-210705/.

Author Photo

Marissa Both, photographer

ABOUT THE AUTHOR

Joshua Rivedal is the creator and founder of Changing Minds: A Mental Health Based Curriculum and The i'Mpossible Project. He has a B.S. in Business Administration with a focus in Organizational Psychology (*summa cum laude*) from Southern New Hampshire University and is trained in community counseling from the Southern California Counseling Center, human capital management with an emphasis in coaching from NYU, QPR, ASIST, and the teacher's edition of emotional intelligence at Yale University's Center for Emotional Intelligence. He has spoken about suicide prevention and mental health across the U.S., Canada, the U.K., and Australia. His original coursework on suicide prevention is taught in Washington State to various professions, such as dentists, pharmacists, and occupational therapists. He wrote and developed the one-man play, *Kicking My Blue Genes in The Butt*, which has toured extensively throughout the world paired with suicide prevention education. His memoir *The Gospel*

According to Josh: A 28-Year Gentile Bar Mitzvah is on The American Foundation for Suicide Prevention's recommended reading list. His second book, The i'Mpossible Project: Volume 1—*Reengaging with Life, Creating a New You*, debuted #1 in its category on Amazon in January 2016. There are currently five books in the i'Mpossible Project series. He is a co-author of three journal papers, one on the trajectory of the survivor of suicide loss, another on the art of living with chronic illness, and the third on surviving trauma. He has a certificate in food, nutrition, and health from the Community College of Philadelphia. Joshua practices Taekwondo and achieved the rank of 1st-degree black belt. As an actor, Joshua's voice has been heard on U.S. national commercials like Dell, McDonald's, Dunkin Donuts, and Johnnie Walker; on one of the Freckleface Strawberry Books, *Cinderella Penguin*, and as part of the award-winning voiceover cast of *The Art of Secrets* by James Klise. He is a standup comic and cook and lives in Philadelphia, Pennsylvania. www.iampossibleproject.com

www.ingramcontent.com/pod-product-compliance
Lightning Source LLC
Chambersburg PA
CBHW031124080526
44587CB00011B/1105